KILLING
FANNIN

The Palm Sunday Massacre of 390 Prisoners at Goliad

ROY SULLIVAN

authorHOUSE®

AuthorHouse™
1663 Liberty Drive
Bloomington, IN 47403
www.authorhouse.com
Phone: 1 (800) 839-8640

Published by AuthorHouse 08/17/2018

ISBN: 978-1-5462-5588-8 (sc)
ISBN: 978-1-5462-5587-1 (e)

Print information available on the last page.

This book is printed on acid-free paper.

Dedicated to Nancy: co-conspirator, editor, critic and photographer

Author Note: Although lacking footnotes, this story of the events leading to the Goliad massacre of some 390 unarmed Texas/volunteer prisoners of war (and their commander, Colonel James W. Fannin, Jr.) on Palm Sunday, March 27, 1836, by the Mexican Army is true.

Sometimes history depends on the opinions of subject experts long time after the event; other times on the perhaps more objective recollection of eye witnesses. Unlike the Alamo where all the defenders were killed, the Goliad massacre had several survivors. Their memories and records—bloody, brutal, perhaps ungrammatical and misspelled—recall this horrifying episode in the history of the Texas Revolution.

CONTENTS

ILLUSTRATIONS AND UNFAMILIAR TERMS

Illustrations:

Unfamiliar Terms:

Alcalde- Spanish for Mayor
Bexar (or Bejar)- the county containing San Antonio, Texas
CPL- a Corporal
CPT- a Captain, usually the commander of a company-sized unit
Capitulation- surrender
Centralist- supporter of Santa Anna's dictatorial government which discarded the
liberal Mexican Constitution of 1824
Dragoons- mounted infantry of the Mexican Army
Execution- death as a legal penalty
1SGT- the rank of First Sergeant, the senior noncommissioned officer of a company
KIA- killed in action
LT- a Lieutenant, usually a platoon leader in a company
League- approximately three miles
Massacre- atrocious killing of unarmed, unresisting individuals
Murder- killing a person unlawfully, usually with malice
POW- prisoner of war
Rancheros- South Texas ranchers supporting Santa Anna
Scopets- shotguns, from the Spanish "escopetas"
"Sentinel Alerto!"- the cry of a Mexican guard reporting he is awake and alertSurrender at discretion- unconditional surrender without terms or reservations
Tejanos- Texans of Mexican heritage

Volunteers/insurgents- Texans and Americans fighting for Texas independence

WIA- wounded in action

XO- executive officer, second in command of a company or battalion

RECOMMENDED READING

Barnard, J.H., "Dr. J.H. Barnard's Journal," contained as Appendix 1 in Clarence Wharton's "Remember Goliad." (see below)

Brands, H.W., "Lone Star Nation," New York, NY: Doubleday, 2004.

Brown, Gary, "James Walker Fannin," Plano, TX: Republic of Texas Press, 1945.

Brown, John H., "History of Texas," Austin, TX: Jenkins Book Pub.Co., 1970,

De Bruhl, Marshall, "Sword of San Jacinto," New York, NY: Random House, 1993.

Fehrenbach, T.R., "Lone Star," New York, NY: American Legacy Press, 1983.

Field, James H. "Three Years in Texas," Austin, TX: The Steck Company, 1935.

The Handbook of Texas Online, "The Goliad Massacre," Texas State Historical Association.

Handbook of Texas, Austin, TX: Texas State Historical Association, 1952.

Hardin, Stephen L. "Texian Iliad," Austin, TX: University of Texas Press, 1994.

"Men of Goliad Index," Sons of DeWitt Colony, TX.

Michener, James A., "Texas," New York, NY: Random House, 1985.

Moore, Stephen L., "Rising Texas," New York, NY: Harper Collins, 2015.

O'Connor, Katheryn S., "Presidio La Bahia," Austin, TX: Von Boeckmann-
Jones, 1966.

Roell, Craig H. "Remember Goliad!" Austin, TX: Texas State Historical Association, 1994.

Shackelford, Jack, "Massacre at Goliad-Captain Jack Shackelford's Account,"
Sons of DeWitt Colony, TX.

Stout, Jay A., "Slaughter at Goliad," Annapolis, MY: Navy Institute Press, 2008.

Sullivan, Roy F., "The Texas Revolution: Tejano Heroes," Bloomington, IN:
AuthorHouse, 2011.

Urrea, Jose de, "Diary of the Military Operations of the Division," Sons of DeWitt Colony, TX.

Wharton, Clarence, "Remember Goliad!" Glorieta, New Mexico: The Rio Grande Press, 1968.

REVOLUTIONARY TEJAS

RIVERS
1 - Sabine
2 - Brazos
3 - Colorado
4 - Guadalupe
5 - San Antonio
6 - Nueces
7 - Rio Grande

BATTLE SITES, OTHER LOCATIONS
A - Nacogdoches
B - Anahuac
C - Lynch's Ferry
D - San Jacinto
E - Galveston
F - Washington-on-the-Brazos
G - San Felipe
H - Harrisburg
I - Velasco
J - Gonzales
K - Victoria
L - San Antonio
M - The Alamo
N - Mission Concepcion
P - Goliad
O - Refugio
Q - Copano
R - San Patricio
S - Agua Dulce
T - Matamoros

(1 inch = approx. 100 miles)

Photo courtesy NK Rogers

CHAPTER 1

CHAOTIC TEXAS IN 1836

" Texas?" It was legally still a part of Mexico, just a *portion* of the Mexican state known as "Coahuila y Tejas," then headquartered at Monclova, Coahuila, Mexico.

The infant Texas faced a myriad of daunting problems. Its populace was an amalgam of old-time colonists who settled in its several colonies, like that of colonizer/entrepreneur Stephen F. Austin, the "Father of Texas."

Plus two other disparate groups.

Other old timers included the many Mexican-Texans (Tejanos) some of whose roots could be traced to the colonial Spanish era.

A third group was the newest and loudest: "Texians" (now called Texans) and volunteers lured there by a sense of adventure and generous land grants from the Mexican government for settlers. Many of the newcomers demanded Texas be free from Mexican (read Santa Anna's dictatorial) domination. Volunteer military units from Louisiana, Tennessee, Kentucky and Georgia began organizing back in their home states and making their way to Texas overland or through Gulf ports like Copano, near Goliad.

Their goal was the independence of Texas.

Texas' initial governing body was the Consultation organized in November, 1835 and attended by Sam Houston. The Consultation delegates preferred Texas be an integral part of the Mexican federation instead of being twinned with the state of Coahuila. As the Consultation evolved into a larger body called the Convention, the goal changed. Now an independent Texas became the objective or even eventual union with the United States. Called the "General Convention" (one member of which was again fiery Sam Houston), there was little consensus, comity, even coordination. The Convention was headed by Governor Henry Smith, himself about to be impeached and replaced by Lieutenant Governor Robinson.

Texas independence would require a trained, adequately equipped and provisioned army to face the much larger, better armed, equipped and experienced army of Mexican President and General-in-Chief Antonio Lopez de Santa Anna.

The new Texas Army needed an experienced, capable Commander-in-Chief able to direct both his fledgling army plus deal with the political antics of an equally new, unsteady government.

An example of the Convention's lack of

coordination: at one time it appointed not just one but *five* Commanders-in-Chief.

Among them was the doughty Sam Houston, late of the Tennessee militia and the Cherokee Nation. Another designated commander was James Fannin, an undistinguished, never-graduated or commissioned former cadet of the U.S. Military Academy at West Point.

Frank W. Johnson, commanded some of the volunteers eventually routing Mexican General Martin Perfecto de Cos and his army from Bexar (San Antonio). Another designated commander-in chief was a formerly wealthy landowner from Northern Mexico, Doctor James Grant, anxious to regain some of his lost Mexican wealth. Grant was an advocate of capturing Mexico's important gateway city of Matamoros, an effort he was anxious to personally lead.

Yet another officer, already in command at the soon-to-be-besieged Alamo in San Antonio de Bexar, was Lieutenant Colonel William B. Travis, busily improving the defenses and attracting volunteers to the venerable old mission's meager garrison of 150 men.

Volunteers, the majority of those fighting for Texas independence, were a breed of their own. Some were individuals with families and jobs which called them away for emergencies or crops, followed by eventual return to their units. Regulations, spit and polish, discipline were anathema to most volunteers, used to electing their officers.

Soldiers—both volunteer and regular—were offered little incentive to serve in the "Provisional

Texas Army" other than patriotism. Food, uniforms, pay, even gunpowder and lead for their deadly long rifles were scarce, sometimes nonexistent.

The differences between regulars and volunteers were a particular problem at the Alamo until Travis (a regular officer) eventually agreed to share command responsibilities with the famous knife-fighter and popular volunteer commander, James Bowie.

Fannin as a Young West Point Cadet, circa 1820
Photo courtesy NK Rogers

CHAPTER 2

JAMES WALKER FANNIN, Jr.

James Fannin (sometimes spelled Fanning) was born in Georgia, probably in early 1804, the illegitimate son of Doctor Isham Fannin, a veteran of the War of 1812. James was adopted by his maternal grandfather, James W. Walker. As a fourteen year old youngster, he obtained an appointment to the United States Military Academy at West Point in 1819. The military service of his father (War of 1812) and grandfather (American Revolutionary War) may have aided his application. He enrolled as "James H. Walker," named for his maternal grandfather. After two years at the Academy he resigned, citing family responsibilities for his aging grandparents. His resignation might have been triggered by other reasons: dueling with another cadet and his poor academic standing. Fannin (or Walker) ranked 60 in order of "general merit" among his class of 86. His record also indicated frequent punishment for being absent or late for classes and formations.

Returning to his home in Georgia, he became a merchant and married the love of his life, Minerva Fort. They had two daughters, Missouri Pinckney and Minerva. Opportunities in Texas beckoned and the Fannins moved there in 1834. He became a plantation owner near Velasco when not engaging in the nefarious slave trade. On just one voyage to Cuba in June, 1835, he illegally brought 153 slaves to Texas. Sometimes Fannin off-loaded slaves at a point on the San Bernard River called "Africans' Landing."

"Committees of Safety and Correspondence" were organized among colonists and newcomers to further the revolutionary cause against Santa Anna's government. Not only was Fannin attracted to this movement, he was appointed a "confidential agent" by such a committee. The appointing agent addressed him as "Colonel" to which rank failed cadet Fannin felt entitled for the rest of his life.

It wasn't long until he organized a small company of volunteers called the Brazos Guards which he led to Gonzales, site of a successful October 2 skirmish with Mexican troops seeking the return of a cannon loaned to Gonzales for defense against Indians.

Also on October 2, Fannin joined others in a published, biblical appeal for armed help at Gonzales:

"Fellow Citizens:

We…urge as many as can be possibly leave their homes to repair to Gonzales immediately, 'armed and equipped for war even to the knife.'…If Texas will now act promptly; she will soon be redeemed from that worse than Egyptian bondage which now cramps her resources and retards her prosperity.

J.W. Fannin, Jr. (et al)"

Gonzales became the "Lexington of the Texas Revolution," famed for its homemade flag—black cannon on a white background—and challenging motto *"Come and Take It."* (referring to the small cannon the retreating Mexicans were unable to recover.)

An advocate of Texas independence, Fannin next assisted the famous and fabled Jim Bowie in scouting the Bexar (San Antonio) area for a suitable base of operations for General Stephen F. Austin's small Texas Army. Their selection was an old Spanish Mission called Concepcion, just south of town. Austin intended to gather his forces there to defeat his opponent, Mexican General Cos, whose army occupied San Antonio.

On October 27, Jim Bowie led a 92 man "patrol" accompanied by Fannin and Captain Juan Seguin, in search of a suitable base of operations for General Stephen F. Austin's offensive against General Martin Perfecto de Cos.

Starting at Mission Espada, Austin's temporary headquarters, Bowie and company rode up the San Antonio River, next examining another mission called San Juan. Finding it indefensible, they rode further upriver to Mission San Jose, which received the same verdict.

That evening they approached Mission Concepcion and—after examination— claimed it as Austin's new base of operations. It nestled in a 100 yard curve in the San Antonio River, some 500 yards away. The river banks were timbered yet within the curve there were only a few trees, affording a good field of fire for Bowie's sharpshooters. Pleased to find this excellent location and deeming it too late to return to General Austin waiting at Mission Espada, Bowie pitched camp and prepared to defend Concepcion, about two miles from town.

General Cos' scouts were active and soon reported Bowie's presence. Cos ordered 400 men of the Morales Division, containing infantry, cavalry and a six-pound cannon, to attack Bowie during the foggy early morning of October 28.

Bowie's men were well emplaced on an east bank curve next to a small embankment. From the embankment, his riflemen had a clear field of fire at Mexican soldiers crossing the river banks. Additionally, they could fire their rifles at the enemy, slide a few feet down the embankment, safely reload and resume their excellent firing positions.

Riflemen Noah Sedgwick described the fight with the Mexican infantry and cannoneers:

"Three times they charged, but there was a platoon ready to receive them. Three times we picked off their gunners, the last one with a lighted match in his hand; then a panic seized them, and they broke. They jumped on the mules attached to the cannon, two or three to a mule, without even taking time to cut them loose, and struck out for the fort, leaving the loaded gun on the field...We turned their cannon on them, adding wings to their flight. They dropped their muskets, and splashing through the shallow waters, fled helter skelter..."

Unsuccessfully, the Mexicans charged the insurgents three more times, then, discouraged and bloodied, headed back to town. Their losses were ten KIA plus their cannon.

In a short thirty minutes, the battle of Concepcion was over. General Austin led his new army forward to occupy Mission Concepcion and began planning to deploy his troops against Cos and the Mexicans the next day.

"You're making too good a target," Bowie chided Fannin, standing cadet-style beside him, "even for a Mexican shootin' a Brown Bess musket. Git down!"

Sadly, Fannin gained a false—eventually fatal—opinion of the fighting ability of the Mexican *soldado* and his officers from James' limited combat experience at Concepcion and Gonzales.

Later Fannin decided to proselyte for a promotion. He wrote to Major James Kerr, a member of the Consultation's Council, saying "one major general has been elected. (Sam Houston) His command, of course, in a military point of view, would be a division—say two brigades. If two brigades, you should then appoint two brigadier generals...."

In January, Fannin was appointed agent by his fledgling government to raise troops and funds for an ambitious campaign to seize Matamoros, Mexico. He also attempted to recruit serving U.S. Army officers for the Provisional Texas Army.

The Texas General Convention was replaced by a Council which removed General Houston as the Texas Army commander-in-chief. Fannin, as Houston's replacement, was authorized to organize and lead a campaign against Matamoros. Marshalling volunteers at Refugio, Fannin's ambition of becoming a brigadier general looked brighter as more troops were added to his command.

On February 7, 1836, Fannin received an urgent message. The Mexicans were gathering their own invasion force of over 1,000 infantry and cavalry at Matamoros. Lieutenant Placido Benavides, a respected and renowned Tejano supporter of Texas independence, was the source of this disturbing intelligence. If true, it meant Fannin should forget Matamoros, prepare to defend South Texas rather than invade northern Mexico.

Major Robert C. Morris of the Texas Army agreed and added to Benavides' report: Santa Anna vowed he would "Take Texas or Lose Mexico."

Morris left a sad but proud legacy when writing home before he later was killed at Agua Dulce with Dr. Grant.

"I am in a dangerous land and may be knocked over at any time. If so, I leave my lands to my sisters and will leave an immortal name. I have accomplished what I came for in having aided the freedom of Texas."

CHAPTER 3

TEXAS CALLS FOR VOLUNTEERS

L ouisiana was the first state sending volunteers to join the fight for Texas independence. A group calling themselves the New Orleans' Greys met in that city on October 13, 1835, rallying to speeches about arming and aiding their brothers in Texas, just across the Sabine River. The meeting was a success: 115 men volunteered to fight for Texas. More than five thousand dollars were donated to equip and arm the "Greys," named for the predominate color of their uniforms. The New Orleans' Greys were the first such volunteers to actually fight. They helped force Mexican General Martin Perfecto de Cos and his army from Bexar (San Antonio), eventually out of Texas. Cos' retreat was halted and reversed by his angry brother-in-law, Antonio Lopez de Santa Anna, President of Mexico and general-in-chief of its vast army. Several New Orleans' Greys fought for Texas with distinction at several battles including the Alamo,

San Patricio, Agua Dulce, Refugio, Coleto, Goliad, and even San Jacinto.

In November 12, 1835, a similar group gathered in Macon, Georgia, to further the cause of Texas independence. The meeting's success encouraged similar meetings about Texas in other Georgia towns like Columbus and Milledgeville. Enthusiasm sparked by the Macon muster translated into 32 "enlistments" and more than three thousand dollars in donations. By the end of November, the number of volunteers heading for Texas increased to 80 men. William Ward, a Macon landowner and slaveholder, was elected their commander.

In Courtland, Alabama, Jack Shackelford, a local doctor and entrepreneur, also began organizing a company to serve in Texas. Fifty-five volunteers signed up and over one thousand dollars collected. The company was dubbed the Red Rovers because of their red uniform trousers made by local wives. Fringed checked shirts and a red flag completed their kit. The Red Rovers left Courtland on December 12, 1835, bound for Texas.

Other Alabamans responded to Sam Houston's plea, printed in the Huntsville, Alabama, *Democrat:*

"Let each man come with a good rifle and 100 rounds of ammunition—and come soon. Our war-cry is 'Liberty or Death.' Our principles are to support the Constitution, and DOWN WITH THE USURPER!" (Santa Anna)

Three other groups from Alabama responded. Huntsville sent 20 men, which number swelled to 70 by the time they reached Texas. A group called the Alabama Greys, 40 men, departed from Montgomery. Not to be outdone, the Mobile Greys, another 35 men arrived in Texas, bound for Goliad, by November.

The largest initial group of volunteers, this the Georgia Battalion of Permanent Volunteers commanded by Lieutenant Colonel William Ward, landed at Velasco, Texas, on December 10. Notably the weapons of the Georgia Battalion were provided by the State of Georgia and the Georgia State armory. Most other volunteer units were armed and equipped through generous private donations. Ten days before the Georgia Battalion arrived in Texas, the Alamo had fallen on March 6. Lieutenant Colonel William Travis and his small force of approximately 200 men were annihilated by Santa Anna's 1800 soldiers that day.

CHAPTER 4

SANTA ANNA'S DEATH THREAT

T here was another disturbing date.

Santa Anna made clear his intention regarding the rebellion in Texas. Armed foreigners "shall be treated and punished as pirates," meaning death, no quarter. A harsh December 30, 1835, decree—instigated by President Santa Anna—was issued by Minister of Defense and Marine Jose Maria de Tornel. In short, the Tornel decree stated:

"1st. All foreigners who disembark in any port of the Republic, or enter it by land, in arms, and with the object of attacking our territory, shall be treated and punished as pirates, in consideration of their not belonging to any nation with which the Republic is at war, and of their not flying any recognized flag.

2nd. All foreigners who may disembark in any port or introduce by land arms and munitions destined for any district in revolt against the National Government, with the known object of placing such means of warfare in the hands of the enemy, shall be treated and punished in the same manner."

Santa Anna's cruelty, even to his own people, was well known. When the silver-rich state of Zacatecas revolted against his centralist government, he sent in the army to break and bloody the rebellion. Two hundred-fifty Zacatecans were killed during the savagery and more than 2,700 were captured. The army—many of whom were convicts—was allowed to sack, pillage, loot and rape the populace as a severe and lasting lesson. Were this not enough punishment, a chunk of Zacatecas' territory was ceded to a new state, Aguas Calientes.

In November, 1835, Santa Anna ordered 27 prisoners executed from General Jose Antonio Mexia's ill-fated campaign to capture Tampico, Mexico. The executed men had been recruited by Mexia in New Orleans.

The lessons of Zacatecas and Tampico should have horrified Texas and Louisiana, as well as all Americans. Santa Anna was eager to repeat these outrages in Texas.

Later, on April 6, 1836, a law was passed in Mexico making the above decree even plainer. The punishment for prisoners of war captured in Texas would be death.

In just three months, Santa Anna would use these cruel measures to justify the deaths of all the Alamo defenders and the massacre of insurgent prisoners of war, many of them wounded, captured throughout South Texas, Coleto and Goliad.

CHAPTER 5

THE LAFAYETTE BATTALION
OF VOLUNTEERS

Among this battalion's companies was the Mobile Greys, organized in Mobile, Alabama, in November, 1835. One of its organizers was Lieutenant James B. Bonham, later famed for his brave dashes in and out of the besieged Alamo to unsuccessfully request reinforcements from Fannin and elsewhere. Originally the Mobile Greys numbered only thirty, commanded by David N. Burke, and arrived in Bexar a few days after General Cos' December surrender and retreat.

By February 12, a second company of Mobile Greys was at Goliad/La Bahia, becoming a part of Major Benjamin Wallace's Lafayette Battalion, thus part of Fannin's regiment. The Mobile Greys were joined by approximately 20 members of the New Orleans' Greys.

The Mobile Greys

Commander: CPT. David N. Burke; XO: 2d LT. J.B. McManomy; 1SGT James Kelly; SGT H.D. Ripley.

John Chew, Jacob Coleman, John D. Cunningham, G.F. Curtman, Randolph De Spain, Neil John Devenney, Samuel M. Edwards, Conrad Eigenauer, Herman Ehrenberg, Micajah G. Frazier, William James Gatlin, William T. Green, Joseph Hopkins, William Hunter, Charles B. Jennings, Thomas Kemp, Montgomery P. King, P.T. Kissam, Charles Linley, Peter Mattem, William McMurray, Zeno R. O'Neil, James Reid, John Richards, William Rosenbury, John Seward, Joseph H. Spohn, William Stevens, Archibald Swords, Kneeland Taylor, Orlando Wheeler, Alvin E. White, William P. Wood.

More "Greys" (also named for the color of their uniforms) joined those from Mobile: the latest additions called themselves the New Orleans' Greys. The first fifty volunteers of the New Orleans' Greys received a new rifle, thanks to the generosity of Alcalde (mayor) Adolphus Sterne of Nacogdoches. Some of the New Orleans' Greys bravely fought at the Alamo (23 KIA), Bexar (1 KIA), San Patricio, Agua Dulce, Refugio, Coleto (21 KIA) and La Bahia. Seven of the surviving New Orleans' Greys even fought at San Jacinto.

Arriving at La Bahia, the New Orleans' Greys intended to continue on to the Alamo and strengthen their brother company of New Orleans' Grays already there. Fannin refused to provide them the necessary supplies and provisions for their march to Bexar. The result was continuing animosity between Fannin and the New Orleans' Greys.

The New Orleans' Greys contingent in the Alamo carried a blue silk banner identifying it as the "First Company of Texan Volunteers from New Orleans." It was presented by a group of local ladies on the outskirts of San Augustine, Texas, where the Greys were welcomed with an official dinner. The blue banner later was captured by the Mexicans when the Alamo fell and the Greys (and all other defenders) killed.

The New Orleans' Greys flag was of singular importance to Santa Anna. It vindicated his assertion that his enemies at the Alamo—and elsewhere—were "pirates." In his report to Mexico City of the Alamo victory, he wrote:

"The inspection of it (the flag) will show plainly the true intentions of the treacherous colonists, and of their abettors, who came from the United States of the North."

Texas' attempts to retrieve the historic flag from Mexico have been unsuccessful.

Adding to the variety of the Lafayette Battalion was Captain Barr Duval's company from Bardstown, Kentucky, dubbed the Kentucky Mustangs.

The Kentucky Mustangs

Commander: CPT. Burr H. Duvall; LT.s Samuel Wilson; William Jefferson Merrifield; SGT.s George Washington Daniel; James S. Bagby; Enoch P. Gaines Chisum; William P. Dickerman; CPLs Norborne B. Hawkins; Abner B. Williams; A.H. Lynd; Richard C. Brashear; Dr William H. Magee.

James Moss Adams, Thomas G. Allen, James B. Batts, Fred J. Bellows, John Van Bibber, William S. Carlson, Thomas T. Churchill, William H. Cole, John Donohoo, H.M. Downman, John Crittenden Duval, George Dyer, Charles Ready Haskell, John C. Holliday, Edward J. Johnson, James P. Kemp, Adams G. Lamond, William Mason, James A. McDonald, William Mayer, Harvey Martin, Robert Smith Owings. Robert R. Rainey, Charles B. Shain, Augustus V. Sharpe, Samuel Smith Sanders, Lawson S. Simpson, Lewis Tilson, B. W. Tolover, J.Q. Volckner, William Waggoner, Ulrich Wuthrich.

Another small company assigned to the Lafayette Battalion was also called "Greys," this one from San Antonio. Captain Samuel Pettus commanded the San Antonio Greys, some 41 men strong.

The San Antonio Greys

Commander: CPT. Samuel O. Pettus; CPT. Benjamin H. Holland, Artillery; XO: LT. John C. Grace; SGT.s Ebenezer Smith Heath; James, Samuel Riddell, William L. Hunter.

William Brenan, Nathaniel R. Brister, A. Bynum, Mariano Carbajal, Charles J. Carriere, J.M. Cass, Henderson Cozart, Noah Dickinson, Jr., Escott, George M. Gilland, Gould, Francis H. Gray, George Green, Milton Irish, William Harper, Stuart Hill, Nathan Hodge, James Noland, David J. Jones, W.P. Johnson, Allen O. Kinney, John C. Logan, Dennis Mahoney, Edward Mooney, D.A.J. Perkins, Charles Phillips, William G. Preusch, John Rees, Joseph P. Riddle, Charles Sargent, R.J. Scott, Wallace, James West, John Wood.

There were yet more Greys, this one largely from Huntsville, Alabama, and commanded by Captain Benjamin Bradford.

More volunteers from Alabama came to Texas to fight in the Lafayette Battalion. This was a large company named the Red Rovers because of the color of their trousers. Their commander was Captain Jack Shackelford, also a physician, who became an outspoken critic—once admirer—of Fannin, his ambitious regimental commander.

The Alabama Red Rovers

Commander: CPT. Jack Shackelford; 1 LT. Francis S. Early; Orderly SGT. Fortunatus S. Shackelford; 2 SGT. Isaac D. Hamilton; 3 SGT. A.G. Foley; 4 SGT. Zachariah H. Short; 1 CPL. Henry Hogue; 2 CPL. David Moore; 3 CPL. John H. Barkley; 4 CPL. Andrew Winter; Dr. John Walker Baylor.

Patrick H. Anderson, John N. Barnhill, Joseph H. Blackwell, Zachariah S. Brooks, Thomas Burbridge, Benjamin F. Burt, J.W. Cain, Seth Clark, John G. Coe, Dillard Cooper, Harvey Cox, Robert T. Davidson, George A. Davis, H.B. Day, Abijah Hogan Dickson, Alfred Dorsey, Henry L. Douglas, William G. Douglas, James W. Duncan, James E. Ellis, Samuel Farney, Robert Fenner, Joseph E. Ferguson, Elijah B. Franklin, David Gamble, M.C. Gardner, James H. Grimes, William Gunter, William Hemphill, John Heyser, Henry W. Jones, John Jackson, John N. Jackson, John Kelly, Charles W. Kinley, Isaac H. Miller, David A. Murdock, William Quinn, William F. Savage, J.M. Seaton, William Shackelford, Wilson Simpson, Bennett Strunk, Simpson Tennant, W.E. Vaughn, James Vaughn, James S. Wilder, Robert W. Wilson.

Added to the Lafayette Battalion was Captain Westover's artillery battery of regulars, long-time occupants of Goliad's Presidio La Bahia, now renamed Fort Defiance by Fannin.

Captain Westover's Company of Regulars

Commander: CPT. Ira J. Westover; XO. 1LT. Francis W. Thornton; 2 LT. Lucias W. Gates; 3 LT. Bennett McNelly; 1SGT. William S. Brown; 3 SGT. John McGoin.

Augustus Baker, Marvin Bell, Marion Betts, Andrew Michael Boyle, Daniel Buckley, Matthew Byme, G.W. Coglan, Matthew Conway, John Cross, George Dedrich, Richard Desney/Disney, Andrew H. Eddy, Matthew Eddy, Otis G. Eels/Eiles, Robert English, John Fadden/Fadder, Edward Garner, John Gleeson, E.J.D.Grinolds, William Harris, William R. Hatfield, John Hitchard, John Kelly, William H. Mann, Dennis McGowan, Patrick Neven, John Numlin, Stephen Pierce, George Pittuck, Edward Ryan, Lewis Shotts, Sidney Smith, Charles B. Stewart, Daniel Syers, Joseph W. Watson, James Webb, William S. Winningham.

Coming from both Paducah, Kentucky, and Huntsville, Alabama, was Captain Peyton Wyatt's company, called the Louisville Volunteers. Command responsibilities were split: the Alabamans were under Lt. Benjamin Bradford, while Kentuckians were under Captain Amon King. This unit was armed with muskets borrowed from the State of Alabama arsenal.

CPT. Wyatt's Company (Louisville Volunteers)

Commander: CPT. Peyton S. Wyatt; CPT. Amon King; CPT. A. Adolph Petrussewicz (Arty); CPT. H. Francis Petrussewicz/Petrewich, (Arty); LT. Benjamin F. Bradford; 2 SGT. George W. Thaye; 3 SGT. Henry Wilkey; Quartermaster Oliver Brown; Musician Peter Allen.

Alfred Allison, Gabriel Bouch, Bennett Butler, Ewing Caruthers, Napoleon Debicki, Henry H. Dickson, Terrell R. Frizzel, John H. Fisher, Edward Fuller, Imanuel F. Giebenrath, James A. Hamilton, Erasmus D. Harrison, John Kornickey, Alexander McLennan, Claiborne D. Mixon, John H. Morgan, John K. Parker, William S. Parker, Charles Patton, Frederick Severunan, John Tyler, Allen B. Wren.

To further add to the Lafayette Battalion's strength was Captain Hugh Fraser's Militia Company of approximately 40 men.

Fraser's Militia Company

Commander: CPT. Hugh M. Fraser; 1LT. John Keating; 2LT. Walter Lambert; 2 SGT. George McKnight.

John W. Bower, Elkanah Brush, James W. Byrnes, Robert M. Carlisle, John Coughlin, Andrew Devereaux, Francis Dietrich, John Fagan, Nicholas

Fagan, Edward Fitzgerald, John James, Peter Hynes, John Keating, Walter Lambert, Victor Loupe, Charles Malone, Edward McDonough, George McKnight, Morgon O'Brien, Thomas O'Connor, Michael O'Donnell, Edward Perry, John Pollen, James Power, Thomas Quirk, Isaac Robertson/Robinson, Antonio Sayle/Siler, Charles Shingle, Edmond St. John, James St. John, William St. John, Anthony Sideck/Sydick, John B. Sideck/Sydick, Martin Toole.,

CHAPTER 6

GEORGIA BATTALION OF PERMANENT VOLUNTEERS

O n its way to New Orleans, this battalion paused in Knoxville, Georgia, to receive a handsome silk banner made by a local lady, Joanna Troutman. The flag was white, containing a single five-pointed blue star with the words "Liberty or Death." This flag and its star kindled the "Lone Star" symbol of the Texas revolution, the new republic and later state.

The Georgians marched to Refugio, Texas, to officially organize and elect officers. Initially, the five company commanders of the Georgia Battalion were Isaac Tichnor, Uriah Bullock, James Winn, William Wadsworth and Amon King.

Captain Ticknor's Company

Commander: CPT Isaac Ticknor; 1LT. Memory B. Tatom; 2LT. William A. Smith; 2 SGT. Nicholas B.

Waters; 4 SGT. Samuel C. Pittman; 1 CPL. Joseph B. Tatom; 2 CPL. James C. Jack; 3 CPL. Perry Reese; 4 CPL. Thomas Reeves; Musician Thomas Lipscomb.

Layton Allen, William L. Alston, Stephen Baker, James A. Bradford, George W. Carlisle, Cullen Conrad, William P.B. DuBose, Edward Fitzsimons, Hezekiah Frost, Jesse Harris, Henry Hastie, David Johnson, Charles Lantz, Oscar F. Leverett, A.M. Lynch, John McGowen, Seaborne A. Mills, Washington Mitchell, Cornelius Rooney, Swords, Evans M. Thomas, James Williams, Isaac N. Wright, James O. Young.

Captain Bullock's Company

Commander: CPT Uriah I. Bullock; 1LT. Basil Lamar; 2 LT. Alexander Patton; 1SGT. Francis M. Hunt; 2 SGT. Bradford Fowler; 3 SGT. Allison Aimes; 4 SGT. Robert Dickinson; 1 CPL. Charles R. Munson; 2 CPL. Thomas S. Freeman; 3 CPL. Samuel T. Bown; 4 CPL George M. Vigal.

Isaac Aldridge, George J. Bridgeman, William A.J. Brown, Munroe Bullock, Moses Butler, George W. Cumming, Joseph Dennis, Michael Devereaux, Michael Ellis, Charles Fine, John Gibbs, James McCoy, Kenneth McKenzie, Drury H. Minor, John Moat, John O. Moore, Robert A. Pace, Austin Perkins, Samuel Rowe, John S. Scully, John Sealy,

Thomas Smith (Abel Morgan), John T. Spillers, Joseph A. Stovall, William Wilkerson, Joseph T. Williams, Henry H. Wood.

Captain Winn's Company

Commander: CPT. James C. Winn. 1LT. Wiley Hughes; 1SGT. Anthony Bates; 2 SGT. John S. Thom; 4 SGT. Wesley Hughes; 1 CPL. John M. Gimble; 2 CPL. Walter W. Daws; 3 CPL. Abraham Stevens; 4 CPL. John M. Powers; CPL. Ray. John Aldridge.

Reason Banks, John Barton, Josias B. Beall, John M. Byson, Michael Carrol, Thomas H. Crosby, John Ely, George Eubanks, Dominic Gallagher, Wilson Helms, Green Lee, Alexander J. Loverly, Joseph S. Loving, S. Mangum, Watkins Nobles, John M. Oliver, Patrick Osburn, William Parvin, Thomas Rumley, Henry L. Shultz, James Smith, John Williams, Harrison Young.

Captain Wadsworth's Company

Commander: CPT. William A.O. Wadsworth; 1LT. Thomas B. Rees; 1SGT. John Smith; 2 SGT. Samuel A.J. Mays; 3 SGT. Samuel P. Wallace; 1 CPL. Josiah (James) McSherry; 2 CPL. J.S. Brown; 4 CPL. Amos D. Kenyon.

Wiley A. Abercrombie, Thomas Barton, Joseph H. Clark, William J. Colson, J.A. Foster, Charles Frazier, William W. Frazier, William Gilbert, Francis Gilkison, Joseph Gramble, Charles C. Milne, John H. Moore, J.H. Saunders, S. Simmons, R. Slatter, Benjamin A. Taliaferro, Wilkins S. Turbeville, Edward Wingate, Solomon Youngblood.

Captain Horton's Mounted Rangers

Commander: CPT Albert C. Horton; LT. James W. Moore; 1SGT. Thomas M. Blake.

Thomas J. Adams, Norman Austin, Jacob Betts, Garrett E. Boom, George Whitfield Brooks, J.W. Buckner, Thomas Cantwell, George W. Cash, Joseph Clements, Thomas J. Dasher, Lewis DeMoss, William DeMoss, J.E. Duffield, Nicholas M. Eastland, Joseph Fenner, William C. Francis, Ransome O. Graves, Jefferson George, William Haddin, John J. Hand, Francis Jones, John Jones, Augustus S. Kincheloe, Daniel Martindale, Charles Morgan, John L. Osborn, Thomas Osborn, George W. Paine, Lewis Powell, Michael Riley, George N. Robinson, Levi Pendleton Scott, Henry Spencer, Christopher Terrell, Thomas S. Thompson, George W. Wheelwright, Napoleon B. Williams, Hughes Witt, Ralph Wright, Elias R. Yeamans, Erastus Yeamans.

Another company, this one from Alabama, was later added to the battalion.

At Refugio, the Georgia Battalion was a welcomed addition to the regiment being organized by its aspiring-to-be brigadier general, James Walker Fannin. He initially planned to lead an expedition into Mexico to seize the city of Matamoros, thus hopefully disrupt Santa Anna's plan to invade Texas.

General Houston criticized the Matamoros expedition with a plain but astute question:

"How can Matamoros" angry twelve thousand inhabitants be defeated by a "handful of men who have marched twenty-two days without bread-stuffs?"

Learning of the approach of Mexican General Urrea (reputedly Santa Anna's best general), Fannin changed his plans. The fortress at Goliad commanded an obvious major objective for the fast-moving Urrea, intent on clearing insurgents from the Gulf coast corridor. On February 25, Fannin led his command—then only about 250 men strong—north to Goliad, some 25 miles away.

Western View of Presidio La Bahia's Wall and Chapel
Photo courtesy NK Rogers

CHAPTER 7

FANNON CONSOLIDATES AT GOLIAD/LA BAHIA

O rganizing the two dissimilar battalions into a cohesive combat-ready command (the First Regiment Texas Volunteers) was a daunting task for Fannin, his staff, the two battalion commanders and their staffs.

Provisional; Regiment of Volunteers

Commander: COL. James W. Fannin; XO: LTC William Ward; Adjutant General Joseph M. Chadwick; Aide-de-camp John Sowers Brooks; Quartermaster David I. Holt; Asst. QM Lewis M.H. Washington; Commissary James Hughes; Surgeons James Field and James H. Barnard; SGM Gideon Rose.

The Lafayette Battalion

Commander: MAJ Benjamin C. Wallace

The Georgia Battalion

Commander: MAJ Warren J. Mitchell

Among Fannin's first tasks for his growing, largely untested and growing command of approximately 420 men at Goliad was to repair and improve the defenses of the old fortress/presidio known as La Bahia del Espiritu Santo. An attack of La Bahia from one of Santa Anna's best generals, General of Brigade Jose de Urrea, already on the long march from Matamoros, could be expected at any time.

There was a festering morale problem. The volunteers had come to Texas to fight Mexicans, not rebuild an old Spanish mission. Fannin faced daily insubordination—which could have developed into mutiny—from his volunteers. His hesitancy and excuses about not immediately marching to the relief of the Alamo did little to solve the problem.

Despite this threat, it was a proud, prestigious period for Fannin. On February 7, he was elected "Colonel of the Provisional Regiment of Volunteers."

The La Bahia mission was near the Gulf, straddling a major approach to east Texas. It was also on commanding terrain overlooking the San Antonio River and a horseshoe curve, about two miles across and five miles across. La Bahia stands on the outer rim of the curve. The old mission was square-shaped with ten foot stone walls surrounding some 3.5 acres. Troop billets were available on two of the four sides of the mission with a small chapel called "Our Lady of Mount Loreto" on the north wall, facing west.

Fannin began a lengthy letter of complaint to the provisional government at ten o'clock one evening, not completed until seven the next morning. The letter derided Texas settlers for their indifference and apathy in not defending their country. Fannin would be a frequent correspondent to Governors Smith, then his replacement, James Robinson.

Later that morning, Fannin inspected his new domain with Joseph Chadwick, who was both his Adjutant General and Engineer.

"What do you think?" Fannin asked Chadwick, busy taking notes, as they walked the mission's perimeter.

Chadwick wiped his face with a red bandana. "Walls are weak and need lots of reinforcement," was the quick reply. "Luckily we have plenty of rock for that purpose. We're going to need lots of labor, too… hard labor, Colonel."

"You'll have it!" Fannin promised. "I'll ask Colonel Ward to provide you two of his Georgia companies today. Can you handle two companies at once?"

"Easy. I'd like to start with more than two."

Fannin pointed at the walls "You know we have eleven cannon which must be positioned at those corners and on the walls. They'll require strong emplacements to withstand the artillery that Mexican General Urrea is bound to bring up from Matamoros. We need a bastion at each of the southern angles and a covered way to get water from the river."

Just then Quartermaster David Holt arrived to report he was storing corn, salt pork, coffee, lead and gunpowder in the small chapel. "Plenty of provisions for a couple of weeks, Colonel, but the Commissary Officer sez we're going to need more...lots more."

Dismissing the Quartermaster with a "well done," Fannin turned back to his Engineer.

"In a few days, we'll be ready for anything the Mexicans can muster," Fannin boasted. "After a while they'll get discouraged and limp back to Mexico just like that General Cos did at Bexar! We're going to defeat anything the Mexicans throw at us here. I think we'll rename this place 'Fort Defiance.' Sound good?"

Without waiting for a reply, Fannin slapped his side. "We've got to work day and night to be ready for that General Urrea!"

Already at 'Fort Defiance' were Captain Ira Westover's artillery battery of regulars plus a militia company commanded by Captain Hugh McDonald.

Meanwhile, Sam Houston was on his way to confer with his old friend, Cherokee Chief Bowles in East Texas. Houston lived with the Cherokees for several years and married a Cherokee. Houston's peacemaking mission was to persuade the Cherokees to ally with Texas, rather than Mexico, in the coming struggle for independence.

In Houston's absence, Fannin became commander-in-chief of the Texas Army, at least temporarily, from February 12 to March 12.

In a startling confession about his own abilities, the usually ambitious Fannin wrote a February 14 letter to Governor James W. Robinson:

"I am not, *practically*, an experienced commander…I *know*, if you and the council do not, that I am incompetent….I do most earnestly ask you…to relieve me, and make a selection of one possessing all the requisites of a commander."

BATTLE OF COLETO: 2:30 p.m. MARCH 19, 1836

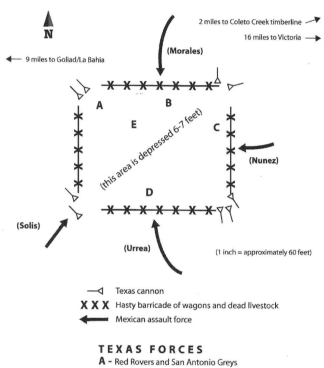

N

2 miles to Coleto Creek timberline →

16 miles to Victoria →

← 9 miles to Goliad/La Bahia

(Morales)

(this area is depressed 6-7 feet)

A

B

E

C

(Nunez)

D

(Solis)

(Urrea)

(1 inch = approximately 60 feet)

◁— Texas cannon

X X X Hasty barricade of wagons and dead livestock

◀— Mexican assault force

TEXAS FORCES
A - Red Rovers and San Antonio Greys
B - Mobile Greys
C - Kentucky Mustangs
D - Westover's Regulars
E - Fannin's position

Photo courtesy NK Rogers

CHAPTER 8

TRAVIS PLEADS FOR ASSISTANCE FROM FANNIN

O n February 18, a young officer from Travis astride a frothing horse rode into Fort Defiance, pleading for assistance for the Alamo. He was Lieutenant James Bonham, one of the original organizers of the Mobile Greys, now a part of the Lafayette Battalion and Fannin's regiment.

The men of Fort Defiance silently listened to Bonham's grim news. "Our side has only a hundred and fifty men in the Alamo," he began. "Santa Anna has nearly two thousand already, with more on the way.

"The odds sound impossible, but with the kind of heroes we have—I mean the determination, the steady fire they're capable of—I believe we can hold the fort till the rest of Texas mobilizes.

"What we need now is for every fighting man in this part of Texas to rush to the Alamo. Strengthen our perimeters! Give us help! Start to march now! The freedom of Texas and the whole United States lies in the balance! Help us!"

Fannin sat, toying with the pommel of his saber during Bonham's impassioned plea. Finally he looked up, smiled and assured the young lieutenant—grimy from his hazardous dark ride through Mexican lines—"I'll think it over."

Angry at Fannin's attitude and response, Bonham remounted his horse and spurred the tired animal toward Victoria where he repeated his plea to a group of farmers.

Note: It is ironic that the seat of Fannin County, Texas, is named for young Lieutenant James Bonham, who pleaded unsuccessfully for Fannin to send reinforcements to Travis at the Alamo. Fannin's service was recognized by this county bearing his name and also a small town near Goliad named Fannin.

Express rider John Johnson reached Goliad on February 25 to deliver Fannin a note from Travis and Bowie:

"We have removed all our men into the Alamo, where we will make such resistance as is due to our honour, and that of the country, until we can get assistance from you, which we expect you to forward immediately. In this extremity, we hope you will send us all the men you can spare promptly. We have one hundred and forty–six men, who are determined *never to retreat*. We have but little provisions, but enough to serve us until you and your men arrive. We deem it unnecessary to repeat to a brave officer, who knows his duty, that we call on him for assistance…"

In reply Fannin pledged that he would march to the Alamo the next morning with 350 men and four cannon. The decision to march to relieve the Alamo was greeted by the volunteers with great enthusiasm. Especially jubilant were the New Orleans' Greys, a company of which already served in the besieged Alamo. Previously, Fannin had denied his Greys the necessary horses and supplies to return to aid their besieged New Orleans' Grey comrades.

Leaving a token force under Captain Westover at La Bahia, Fannin departed the next day with 350 men, marching north along the San Antonio River toward Bexar and the Alamo. After only 200 yards, one wagon broke down and had to be repaired. In a few hundred more yards, two others did the same, near a place to ford the river.

The river was flooded, causing delays in manhandling the cannon across. By afternoon, Fannin decided to establish a camp on the north bank and revaluate his pitiful progress toward the Alamo, still about 25 miles away.

Although the cannon eventually crossed the river, their ammunition had been left on the southern bank due to the raging waters. It was a bleak night at Fannin's campsite on the north bank. It became worse the next morning upon discovery that the oxen pulling the carts had been neither fed nor penned.

Most wandered off during the night. Rounding up the oxen caused another delay.

What did Fannin do? He called a 'conference of officers' to confer, i.e., make a decision for him. Their decision was to "countermarch" back to La Bahia, the starting point less than one mile and a river crossing away.

Herman Ehrenberg, one of the surviving New Orleans' Greys, later castigated Fannin's "countermarch" order by the following:

"Fannin…would neither retreat nor march to the aid of San Antonio, preferring to await the onset of the enemy behind the fortifications he had erected at Goliad. There, at least, he was the undisputed leader, whereas if he returned to the main army he would have to give up his supremacy. With the hope of changing his selfish resolution, we reminded him constantly of the probable fate of our brothers-in-arms if we turned a deaf ear to their appeal. But our efforts were in vain, and vain also were our entreaties imploring him to abandon Goliad. He stuck to Goliad—though to be sure he did not adhere to his course without a struggle. His contradictory orders revealed to us the conflict between his ambition and his generosity…"

Doctor Barnard noted a change in the morale of the men. "The signs of coming danger began to produce a feeling of anxiety, which was further increased by many vague and groundless rumors that circulated among the men. The confinement in the garrison became irksome; our provisions, of which we had at first an abundance, were becoming short;

the restraints of discipline, now more necessary than ever in their enforcement, produced discontent and murmurs and a loss of confidence in their commander."

Meanwhile other riders from the Alamo were enroute to express similar needs. On the dark night of February 29, Tejanos Captain Juan Seguin and Corporal Antonio Cruz managed to evade Mexican sentries and outposts around the Alamo and ride to Goliad. The mission given them by Travis was to request immediate reinforcements from Fannin. The two riders unexpectedly met Captain Francis DeSauque of Fannin's staff outside Bexar. While the three conferred on Cibolo Creek, DeSauque told them that Fannin's relief column was already on the march for the Alamo and should arrive there within two days.

Seguin and Cruz waited for Fannin at the creek. After waiting for some time without a sign of any "relief column," Seguin again tried to relay Travis' message to Fannin.

This time Fannin replied, but through a Lieutenant Finley. He was forced to "countermarch" back to Goliad to defend it because of the approach of General Urrea.

Fannin was correct—not about failing to assist Travis—but about General Urrea's proximity.

This may have been the last time Fannin was absolutely right.

If morale among his men was a problem, it didn't seem to be with Fannin, who boasted February 28:

"I have about 420 men here, and if I can get provisions in tomorrow or the next day, can maintain myself against any force. I will never give up the ship, while there is a pea in the ditch. If I am whipped, it will be *well done.*"

It was during this period that Fannin had misgivings about continuing in command. He repeated an earlier request for an April leave, which he said had been approved:

"I am desirous to be erased from the list of officers, or expectants of office, and have leave to bring off my brave foreign volunteers (the Georgia Battalion), in the best manner I may be able." Particularly, Fannin wanted to rejoin his beloved family.

CHAPTER 9

GENERAL URREA ON THE MOVE

J ose de Urrea was a man of the Houston mold. He was a good tactician, commander, politician, and even a state governor, as had been Houston. Urrea was born in the presidio of Tucson, Sonora, Mexico, (now Arizona) in 1797. By 1809 he was a military cadet and a lieutenant by 1816. For differing political affiliations he was separated from the army but later allowed to reenter service and serve in Tampico. There he met another young ambitious officer named Antonio Lopez de Santa Anna, his future commander-in-chief and several-times president of Mexico.

In 1831 Urrea was promoted to the rank of lieutenant colonel, then to colonel commanding a regiment in 1834. A year later he was an acting general in the state of Durango, next its commandant general and then governor.

General of Brigade Urrea departed Matamoros February 18, leading the Cautla cavalry regiment of about 350 troopers. Also under his command was an infantry battalion from Yucatan containing another 350 soldiers and several militia companies. Urrea left his slower-moving infantry and militia behind as he galloped the cavalry toward the insurgent Texas positions reported by loyal-to-Mexico ranchers (rancheros) in South Texas.

Urrea intended to clear the coastal areas and eliminate the armed insurgents planning to invade Mexico and capture Matamoros behind Santa Anna's back. Receiving excellent intelligence from civilian sources loyal to Mexico, Urrea headed to San Patricio, a small settlement about 50 miles south of Goliad.

San Patricio

The insurgents reportedly there were led by Francis W. Johnson and Dr. James Grant, two of the five Texas Army commanders-in-chief, designated by the hastily organized, fledgling Texas government.

Johnson and Grant and their few men were busily gathering horses from the countryside for use in the planned invasion of Matamoros. A herd gathered by Grant from southern ranches was corralled at the ranch of Julian de la Garza. Johnson and twelve men remained at the Garza spread to guard the horses. Later the twelve guards were increased by arrivals from Dr. Grant's group.

General Urrea's diary (a historical gold mine) for February 27 read as follows:

"I arrived in San Patricio at three in the morning and immediately ordered a party of thirty men headed by Captain Raphael Pretalia to proceed to the ranch of Don Julian de la Garza (a league distant) to attack the twelve or fifteen men who were guarding the horses there.

"I ordered forty dragoons of the remaining force to dismount; and dividing them into three groups under good officers, I gave instructions for them to charge the position of the enemy, protected by the rest of our mounted troops. The enemy was attacked at half past three in the morning in the midst of the rain, andalthough forty men within the fort defended themselves resolutely, the door was forced at dawn, sixteen being killed and twenty-four taken prisoners."

Note: the numbers of KIA and those taken prisoner at San Patricio vary widely. One source (Mexican Lieutenant Colonel Jose de la Pena) indicates 20 KIA and 32 prisoners. Yet another says 10 KIA, 18 prisoners and 6 escapees, including Johnson.

Lieutenant Colonel de la Pena's report on San Patricio noted that six of Urrea's soldiers died of exposure during the bitterly cold approach march. Urrea acknowledged that in one night six soldiers from Yucatan died from the cold. The six, acclimated to warm, tropical Yucatan, were unable to withstand the severe cold weather in South Texas. Pena's account also indicates Urrea lost one dragoon KIA and six wounded at San Patricio.

Agua Dulce

On March 2, Urrea's cavalry located more rebel Texans at the Agua Dulce Creek, 25 miles south of San Patricio. Some twenty-five men, commanded by Dr. James Grant, had been rounding up mounts for the Matamoros expedition. They were ambushed and easily defeated by the Mexicans. Twelve men, including Grant, were killed. Six more were captured and imprisoned in Matamoros. Another six men of Grant's small force escaped to tell Fannin at Goliad the bad news. Another report indicates seven men, not six escaped.

Urrea reported that he killed 40 and took 6 prisoners at Agua Dulce. Again, from his diary, is the following:

"March 1. Still in San Patricio. Received news that Dr. Grant was returning from the Rio Bravo (Rio Grande) with a party of forty or fifty picked riflemen and I marched that night, with eighty dragoons, to meet him. The north wind was very strong and the cold was extreme for which reason I decided to wait for the enemy ten leagues from San Patricio at the port of Los Cuates de Agua Dulce where he would have to pass. I divided my force into six groups and hid them in the woods.

"March 2. Between ten and eleven in the morning Dr. Grant arrived. He was attacked and vanquished by the parties under my command and that of Colonel Francisco Garay. Dr. Grant and forty of the riflemen were left dead on the field and we took six prisoners besides their arms, munitions and horses. I countermarched to San Patricio and sent out new scouts to Goliad."

As ever, reports of Texas casualties differ. Pena reported 42 insurgents killed, which probably included several members of Lieutenant Benavides' Tejano company which had joined Grant's group. Urrea cited "40 riflemen" dead while 12 from Grant's command were listed as KIA.

Many of the Texans were killed quickly in the ambush. Dr. Grant and Rueben Brown charged the Mexicans in a vain attempt to blunt their attack.

Still mounted, Grant and Brown managed to escape but were pursued. About seven miles away, surrounded, they dismounted to fight. Brown was wounded by the lance of a cavalryman whom Grant shot off his horse. Several others ran their lances into Grant. Brown was roped and tied to a horse, to be taken to Matamoros. Before being dragged away, he saw several officers thrusting their sabers into Dr. Grant's body.

Another report was that the Mexicans attached Grant's feet to the back legs of a wild mustang, then tied his hands to the horse's tail. The terrible result was that Grant was kicked to death by the released crazed animal.

Notable among the escapees was First Lieutenant Placido Benavides who commanded his own company during the Texas War of Independence. Benavides yelled to Dr. Grant that Urrea's attacking dragoons had cut the column between themselves and their herd. Benavides wanted to immediately engage the Mexicans but Grant ordered him to escape and ride to Goliad/La Bahia to warn Fannin.

Benavides swiftly rode away to spread the warning about Urrea's presence. First, he sounded a warning to citizens in San Patricio, rode onward to Refugio, then to Goliad where he delivered the sad message to Fannin. Without a rest, Benavides continued to his native town of Victoria with the alarming news of Urrea's presence. For his historic ride through South Texas, warning settlers about Urrea, Benavides is revered as the "Paul Revere of the Texas Revolution."

CHAPTER 10

GENERAL HOUSTON ON THE MOVE

H ouston returned from the Cherokees but not immediately to military duties. Instead he detoured to tiny Washington-on-the-Brazos where the Convention was convening to draft a Texas Declaration of Independence.

Public opinion in Texas previously supported the Mexican Constitution of 1824 and Texas becoming an independent state within the Mexican federation. The Consultation (the pre-Convention Texas government) had reiterated this intent in November, 1835. By the time the Convention convened at tiny Washington-on-the-Brazos on the first of March, 1836, its mood had changed. The delegates now wanted Texas independent of a Mexico dominated by the centralist government of President Antonio Lopez de Santa Anna who had abrogated the Mexican Constitution of 1824.

A draft Texas Declaration of Independence was read aloud to the 41 delegates huddled against the cold in a large, unfinished, open-windowed building on

March 2. The draft was approved, corrections made and the rewritten document signed the next day, March 3, 1836. Houston's name was among the signers.

The declaration concludes with the following:

"We, therefore, the delegates with plenary powers of the people of Texas, in solemn convention assembled, appealing to a candid world for the necessities of our condition, do hereby resolve and declare, that our political connection with the Mexican nation has forever ended, and that the people of Texas do now constitute a free, Sovereign, and independent republic, and are fully invested with all the rights and attributes which properly belong to independent nations; and conscious of the rectitude of our intentions, we fearlessly and confidently commit the issue to the decision of the Supreme arbiter of the destinies of nations."

Delegate Sam Houston applauded the declaration while proudly announcing that the day marked his forty-third birthday. Wily Houston lingered not only for the celebrations and libations, both of which he was fond, but for a written *carte blanche* from the Convention that he was the Commander-in-Chief of *all* Texas forces, volunteers as well as regulars. Houston had seen too often the difficulties dealing with undisciplined volunteers.

Houston should have hurried to Gonzales to begin the daunting task as commander-in-chief to assemble the vestiges of an army to defend the brand new Texas Republic against a powerful and numerically superior enemy already within its gates.

CHAPTER 11

FANNIN SPLITS HIS FORCE, ORDERED TO VICTORIA

On March 10, Fannin received a request from a Refugio family named Ayers to assist its escape from the approaching Mexicans. Apparently that family had not heeded their neighbors' nor Lieutenant Benavides' warnings and had tarried too long in responding to the danger of fast-moving General Urrea.

Concerned about the civilians, Fannin ordered Captain Amon King's Company of the Georgia Battalion to the family's rescue. King took with him 25 soldiers (described as a "company of infantry") and *all* of Fannin's oxen, carts and wagons to transport the family and its possessions to safety.

On the next day, March 11, Houston arrived in Gonzales. He intended to make a long speech to include reading aloud the new Texas Declaration of Independence written at the Convention to which he was a delegate. The citizens of Gonzales gathered at

DeWitt's Tavern to hear the famous former Tennessee governor, politician, soldier and orator.

Houston also planned to read his own appointment order as a major general and Commander-in-Chief of all armed forces of the Republic of Texas. Those forces, Houston emphasized, included the entire Army: militia, volunteers, rangers and regulars.

Before Houston could finish his lengthy speech, two Tejano scouts rode in with the appalling news that the Alamo had fallen and all its defenders—including Travis, Bowie and Crockett—killed.

The effect was immediate and contagious. Remembering what Santa Anna's troops had done to Zacatecas, Texas families began piling belongings on horses and carts. They hurried out of towns and communities as fast as they could, headed for East Texas and Louisiana via the so-called "Sabine chute." Towns were set ablaze as their former inhabitants and livestock herds joined the "Runaway Scrape." How could Texas possibly survive a rampaging, victorious Mexican Army?

Major General Sam Houston quickly found a table, chair and paper to issue an order to Fannin at La Bahia. "You will," Houston wrote, "as soon as practicable after the receipt of this order, fall back upon Guadalupe Victoria, with your command and such artillery as can be brought with expedition. The remainder will be sunk in the river. You will take the necessary measures for the defence of Victoria, and forward one third the number of your effective men to this point, and remain in command until further orders.

"Every facility is to be afforded to women and children who may be desirous of leaving that place. Previous to abandoning Goliad, you will take the necessary measures to blow up the fortress; and do so before leaving its vicinity. The immediate advance of the enemy may be confidently expected, as well as a rise of water. Prompt movements are therefore highly important."

Houston planned that—with the addition of Fannin's force—the Texas Army had a chance to later defeat Santa Anna at a time and place of Houston's choosing.

Couriers David Kent and Ben Highsmith delivered Houston's order to Fannin on the 13th. Anxious to report completion of their mission to Houston, Highsmith asked Fannin if he was going to comply.

"No." Fannin slapped his side for emphasis. "Tell the General I will not give up Fort Defiance."

Why did Fannin disobey Houston's order? Some historians think Fannin awaited the return of Ward and King and their contingents. King had taken all of Fannin's transport on his rescue mission. Other historians attribute Fannin's refusal to obey to his ambition to continue independent command, rather than serve under Houston, whom he probably considered a rival for the eventual presidency of Texas.

Also on the 13th, Houston confided the following to Colonel Henry Raguet in Nacogdoches:

"Colonel Fannin should have relieved our Brave men in the Alamo. He had 430 men with artillery under his command, and had taken up a line of march with a full knowledge of the situation of those in the Alamo, and owing to the breaking down of a waggon abandoned the march, returned to Goliad and left our Spartans to their fate."

Houston added another accusation which sounded remarkably like a court marital charge. "(Fannin)... has already cost us the lives of 230 brave men."

Houston would not know Fannin's full accounting of casualties until later.

> Captain King and his company reached Mission Refugio by March 12, without enemy contact. There he learned of another family in distress and divided his small unit to go to the aid of this second family. Later that same day King was surprised by an armed group of loyal-to-Mexico rancheros led by Carlos de la Garza. The strength of the Garza group variously was reported as 80 to 200 men.

Simultaneously, King's company came under fire from an advance element of Urrea's cavalry. King and his men barricaded themselves in a nearby church, the Mission de Nuestra Senora del Rosario, in Refugio. King immediately sent a messenger to Fannin at La Bahia asking for assistance.

In response, Fannin again fragmented his remaining

La Bahia force by sending Lt. Col. Ward and his Georgia battalion of 125 men to rescue Captain King. On arrival in Refugio, Ward succeeded in scattering the surprised Mexicans besieging King around the church.

Unbelievably, King and Ward began arguing about who was in charge despite their ranks.

Stubbornly, each went his own way. King wanted to punish the rancheros involved, so followed, then ambushed some of them, killing eight. Back at the mission, Ward and his men heard the approach of Mexican cavalry and hurriedly took the place of King's absent men in the mission. The two erring commanders had separated and made their individual forces even smaller instead of returning to La Bahia to join Fannin as the latter ordered.

Captain Jack Shackelford, commander of the Alabama Red Rovers, wrote the following rambling indictment of this incident:

> "About midnight, on the 14th, King's express (message) reached Goliad, and Col. Fannin immediately dispatched Col. Ward's battalion to his relief. *This was the beginning of our trouble* (italics added) and the only act for which I ever blamed Fannin...an unworthy prejudice which has been created in the minds of many, that Fannin wished to forestall Houston in command of the army, and therefore disobeyed his

orders (to destroy La Bahia and march to Victoria)…he committed an error in separating his forces. Had he not done this, we should have been prepared to fall back on Victoria, as ordered, with a force sufficient to contend with every Mexican we might have encountered…"

Urrea arrived at dawn on March 14, surrounded the Refugio mission and assaulted it three times with numerous losses. Inside, Ward's force suffered few casualties but food, water and ammunition were running low. A rider volunteered and succeeded in escaping through the Mexican lines. He headed to La Bahia to tell Fannin of the situation and ask for assistance. Mexican Colonel Francisco Garay, his actions at Agua Dulce mentioned in Urrea's diary, wrote the following concerning his general's mistakes. Dislodging the stubborn Texans defending the Refugio mission proved more difficult than Urrea anticipated:

"The enemy in the number of one hundred men were occupying the church, the only defensible point in that poverty stricken town. This force was cut off at once by the Guanajuato cavalry which anticipated by some moments the arrival of the section. Scarcely was this in sight when they got into battle position in front of the building loosing at once a sortie of thirty men with the purpose of protecting the taking in of two barrels of water which were pulled by oxen, and which the position of the river had concealed from us. This forced the action since the general considered it important to deprive them of this resource, and he gave orders at once, attacking them almost on the instant. Indeed three groups separated and by advancing bravely succeeded in turning back the rebels, taking away from them the water which they were carrying. However, since the latter had also gotten into the church, he did not have the prudence to have our forces withdraw. "Rather to the contrary, he (Urrea) allowed them to advance farther and to remain where they were after exhausting the ammunition of their cartridge belts, the only ones they were carrying, at about thirty yards distant. For a good period of time they were exposed to the accurate fire of the enemy, suffering considerable damage and unable on their part to return the fire. Those in charge of the cannon found themselves obliged to abandon it since it was located so close to the building they could not maintain possession of it. An extraordinary effort was necessary to pull it back, and this was finally done with considerable losses. Although at the beginning only three detachments were sent to attack the enemy, as soon as the latter took refuge in the church, the rest of our foot soldiers got into the fight, and even a part of the Cautla cavalry advanced also on foot. However, it was all in vain. Strong in their position because of our lack of caution, they mocked us with impunity, causing us to pay dearly for our rashness. We had on our part thirteen dead and forty-three wounded, among them four officers, and they had had only one man wounded."

Captain King and his men attempted to return to the Mexican-besieged Refugio mission during the early afternoon but ran into Urrea's rear guard and took cover in a grove of trees next to the Mission

River. There King's sharpshooters inflicted more casualties on Urrea's soldiers.

Fannin's reply to Ward's request for assistance, delivered by the rider, was an order for Ward to fall back to Victoria, where Fannin also had been ordered by Houston. Ward left volunteers with his wounded and the families on the night of the 14th. He chose an escape route toward Copano on the coast, hoping to evade Urrea's cavalry patrols searching for him on the Goliad road. During that night, King and his men also attempted to escape from the mission. They left behind their wounded comrades plus several women and children sheltered there.

King's company crossed the Mission River that night but was discovered by local rancheros loyal to Mexico. When attempting to fight, King discovered to his horror that most of his gunpowder had become wet and useless during the river crossing. Locals then captured King and his men and marched them back to the Refugio mission.

There on March 16 Captain King and his company were executed in the Refugio plaza. Of his group thirty-five were killed in action or executed. Seven or eight were captured but not killed. Among them was Abraham Osborn, spared by Colonel Holzinger from execution due to appeals of a local couple named Cobian.

Note: Holzinger's rank was Lieutenant Colonel but during the later surrender negotiations, General Urrea listed him as a Captain. Holzinger's name was spelled properly with a "z" by the Mexicans, sometimes with an "s" by others.

Another prisoner spared by Holzinger was Lewis T. Ayers of the family Captain King was sent to rescue and evacuate. Ayers described what happened to his would-be-rescuers:

"The rest of our party was barbarously shot, stripped naked, and left on the prairie about one mile from the mission."

Ward evaded capture by heading north for Victoria, only to find the town occupied by the enemy. Some of his group made their way up the coast to Dimitt's Landing on Lavaca Bay. Dismayed, they again found Urrea's men waiting there and surrendered.

Note: The landing is named for Dimitt although his name is Philip Dimmitt.

During its exhausting retreat and escape attempts, Ward's force became marginalized, as seen in the following. Although records are incomplete, Ward's force, originally 120 men, suffered the following:

Seven men lost or escaped near Victoria on March 16

One soldier killed at Victoria on March 21

Ten prisoners executed near Victoria March 21

Ten men left at the Guadalupe River during the night of March 21 and later escaped

Sixteen prisoners detailed by the Mexicans to

build boats at the Guadalupe River, March 23, and later escaped

Five were captured at Victoria and interrogated by General Urrea, but later escaped

Thirty-one men managed to escape capture March 19-20

Thirteen men were captured, sent to Goliad and executed March 27

Two individuals escaped and made their way to Victoria during the night of March 18

By March 16 Ward made it back to Goliad to personally report the failures of King and himself. The news added to Fannin's indecision about obeying Houston's order to retreat and join the main army at Victoria.

Pena critically described the efforts of General Urrea to find, kill or capture the insurgents:

"He ordered Captain Pretalia with a small party of soldiers and thirty fellow townsmen to advance and delay the enemy until he could arrive with a force selected to give battle. He chose 100 horsemen and 180 infantrymen, and with the only field piece he had, started the march; he traveled all night and at dawn on the 14th he found himself facing the enemy, who had been forced to stop at the Mission Refugio... He ordered an assault on the enemy, two hundred in number, who occupied a defensible position. It could not be taken because of the poor infantry destined for the sacrifice, who had been exhausted by the forced marches...The result of General Urrea's attempt was a significant loss to us and none to the enemy except for six wounded."

Pena continued to critique his general. "While he was bent on fighting the force that had entrenched itself in the mission church, another one appeared at his rear guard, compelling him to send part of his reserve to face this new enemy. The latter had deployed himself in a wood, where a creek made him less accessible, so the general had to give up another part of his force."

Needing more firepower to dislodge the Texans in the thick woods, Urrea sent orders to Colonel Francisco Garay to join him as quickly and with all the troops he could muster. Upon Garay's arrival at five in that afternoon, Urrea pointed to the woods occupied by the Texans. Garay attacked the wooded positions and by nightfall the Texans lost five dead and two were taken prisoner. Garay reported his own casualties as three dead and ten wounded.

"Those who remained enclosed (Texans inside the Refugio mission)," Pena continued, "had no food or water, and the general promised that they would surrender the next day or come out in open field and fight. They managed to escape nevertheless... Our losses for this day were eleven dead and thirty-seven wounded, among them, three officers. At dawn on the 15th, when we took possession of the abandoned point we found our wounded, some families of the colonists, and four of the enemy who had chosen not to follow their companions, as well as some compatriots of ours who had been impressed into enemy ranks. The general ordered all the cavalry at his disposal to chase the fugitives, costing the enemy sixteen dead and thirty-one prisoners on this day and fourteen on the following."

Notes: Urrea's men fatally bayoneted two of the wounded volunteers left behind in the mission.

Pena's figure of two hundred Texans in the Refugio mission is high since the total King/Ward force consisted of 28 men with King and 120 with Ward.

Meanwhile, General Urrea claimed a serious morale problem:

"I constantly heard complaints and I perceived the vexation of my troops. I received petitions from the officers asking me to comply with the orders of the general-in-chief and those of the supreme government regarding prisoners. These complaints were more loud on this day (March 16), because, as our position had not improved, *I found myself threatened* (italics added).

"I authorized the execution, after my departure from camp, of thirty adventurers taken prisoner during the previous engagements, setting free those who were colonists or Mexicans."

As expected, Urrea's fellow general, Vincente Filisola, strongly defended Urrea's execution order:

"The war in Texas was exceptional; it was not a civil war; nor was it a war of one nation against another. In it, the thief was fighting against the owner;

the murderer against his benefactor, and nothing was more natural than that these hordes of assassins and thieves should be done away with."

Earlier Houston had ordered Fannin to evacuate Goliad/La Bahia, send a third of his force to the main army and fall back with the remainder to Victoria. The anxious Fannin vacillated, just as he had done about reinforcing Travis at the Alamo. With the loss of the King and Ward contingents, Fannin's force was depleted some 150 men plus most of his precious transport capability.

Fannin continued hoping for the return of some of the carts and oxen taken by King. Transport was badly needed at La Bahia to transport supplies and ammunition. Fannin dispatched more riders to ascertain what happened to Ward and King, but most of them were captured.

Finally, on the afternoon of March 17, Captain Hugh Frazer returned with the chilling news that most of the groups Fannin ordered to Refugio had been killed, captured or were missing. Despite this, Fannin stubbornly intended to remain in his stronghold, La Bahia/Fort Defiance. He may have been influenced by his remaining strength of about 330 men and the recent, considerable strengthening of the fort's defenses.

That same morning, General Houston, unaware that Fannin had not begun withdrawing toward Victoria, issued him a new order. "Take position on Lavaca Bay to protect the army's munitions dumps at

Cox's Point and Dimitt's Landings." Fannin failed to acknowledge or reply.

Captain Horton and his horsemen found some carts and oxen in the vicinity of Victoria and returned them to La Bahia. Relieved that he again had some transport, Fannin called another "council of war." The upshot of this latest council "deliberation" was that La Bahia would be abandoned the following morning, March 18.

More delays resulted in obeying Houston's order to evacuate Fort Defiance/La Bahia/Goliad and withdraw to Victoria. Simultaneously, scouts (probably Horton's) reported the Mexican cavalry was closer than expected, especially to the east of La Bahia. Now alarmed that an attack was imminent, Fannin ordered all the cannon previously buried dug up and readied for service. While making their evening rounds, Fannin and Captain Ira J. Westover paused to question Abel Morgan serving on guard duty. Morgan later recorded their conversation:

"Col. Fanning asked me what I thought about retreating and leaving the fort; I told him that my opinion was that was too late; for I made no doubt from what we had seen that we were entirely surrounded by the enemy, and that we had something like six weeks' provisions and men enough to keep the enemy from breaking in for some time, as we then had about 360 men. Col. Fanning seemed to have his mind unsettled about it. Capt. Westover agreed with me, and said if we had left three or four days before, he thought we might have escaped; but he made no doubt that we were surrounded now."

What a fitful sleep, if any, Fannin must have endured that night.

CHAPTER 12

"PRIOR PLANNING PREVENTS POOR PERFORMANCE"

N o one, commanders, staff officers—even the council of officers Fannin depended upon for decisions—apparently remembered the old adage as they hurriedly prepared to evacuate La Bahia.

Perhaps it was their haste or Fannin's deliberating, stalling and deliberating again before he issued the order to leave Presidio La Bahia. He insisted on packing aboard the few available wagons and carts 500 surplus muskets and extra baggage. Nine towed cannon added to what would become a long, slow march column.

Instead of leaving the fortress during darkness for security and surprise, the column left in broad daylight on the 19th. More delays resulted from Fannin's last minute decision to burn the settlement's houses and to destroy anything of possible value to the Mexicans, including wheat, corn and some 700 beeves recently received from Port Lavaca and other sources.

Billowing smoke testified to the evacuation, probably seen as far away as Victoria. To add to the delay, Mexican cavalry was spotted nearby by Captain Albert C. Horton's mounted troopers who promptly gave chase. For several hours the two sides maneuvered against each other within sight of La Bahia, without casualties. Fannin's soldiers sat upon the presidio walls, enjoying the entertainment.

Captain Shackelford of the Red Rovers, always watchful, noted that "Horton behaved in a very gallant manner, and made a furious charge at the enemy."

Despite mounted charges back and forth by both sides, little was accomplished other than further delay of Fannin's departure. Horton's mounts were exhausted by this exercise in futility. Contrary to Houston's orders, the fortress was not "blown up" prior to departure.

Led by Shackelford's Red Rovers, Fannin, approximately two hundred forty men and the baggage train were finally on their way to Victoria. Duval's Kentucky Mustangs performed as the column's rear guard.

Errors, problems and delays continued. The oxen-pulled carts were heavily overloaded making the hungry oxen stop and graze only a few miles from Goliad. One of the carts broke down and its contents redistributed while it was being repaired. A large cannon rolled into the San Antonio River and had to be heaved out and remounted.

As noon approached, someone hungry noticed that the rations and water had not been loaded. The food had apparently been torched with the beeves and other provisions per Fannin's order.

Despite the many signals that Fannin was finally departing, Urrea's force of some 80 cavalry and 300 infantry did not respond until eleven that morning. By then, Fannin's column—moving only abut two miles an hour—had been on the road since nine o'clock.

CHAPTER 13

TRAPPED AND SURROUNDED IN AN OPEN FIELD

*"We cannot rationally anticipate any other result
to our Quixotic expedition than total defeat."*
John Sowers Brooks, Aide-de-camp of Fannin

N ine miles out of La Bahia, Fannin made another extraordinary mistake. He halted the column for men to rest and oxen to graze. The spot chosen was an expanse of open prairie two miles from a stretch of timber along the Coleto Creek.

Captain/Doctor Jack Shackelford of the Red Rovers made clear his objection to Fannin's choice to stop. "I remonstrated warmly against this measure (halting in the open) and urged the necessity of first reaching the Coleto, then about five miles distant.

"In this matter I was overruled, and from the ardent manner in which I urged the necessity of getting under the protection of timber, I found the smiles many... Col. Fannin and many others could not be made to believe that the Mexicans would dare to follow us. He had too much contempt for their prowess, and too much confidence in the ability of his own little force. That he was deficient in that caution which a prudent officer should always evince, must be admitted; but that he was a brave, gallant, and intrepid officer, none who knew him can doubt."

Another surgeon, Dr. Joseph Barnard, also criticized Fannin's halt. "We ought to have moved at all hazards and all cost until we reached the timber.... We could have moved on and kept them at bay as easily as we repulsed them while stationary."

Fannin disagreed. His previous experience at Concepcion was that the Mexicans were no match for his volunteers. The oxen were unhooked and allowed to graze while the men ate any personal food in their knapsacks and relaxed. After an hour Fannin resumed the slow march toward Victoria, at least ten hours ahead, at their present slow pace.

This time Fannin took the precaution of detailing four young horsemen to perform as look-outs behind the column.

Since Fannin was the only major commander with formal military training, his occasional lapses are curious. One author investigated Fannin's West Point history where he was enrolled as "James Walker" and reported:

"Young James did not perform well, finishing his first year in the bottom half of his class. Partway through his second year, he was put back into the starting class because of his poor academic performance. ...Finally, after more than two years of poor progress, he submitted his resignation on October 25, 1821...While at West Point, he learned little or nothing of the craft of war...Still, in future years these facts would not keep him from claiming that he had acquired great military acumen during his abbreviated stint at West Point."

Nor was Fannin popular with his troops, the malady of many a commander. One of the Alabama Red Rovers, A.J. Ferguson, wrote:

"Our commander is Col. Fannin, and I am sorry to say, the majority of the soldiers do not like him, for what cause I do not know, without it is because they think he has not the interest of the country at heart, or that he wishes to become great without taking the proper steps to attain greatness."

The four horsemen, among them Herman Ehrenburg of the Greys, detailed to watch for the enemy in the rear, halted to graze their mounts and rest. Suddenly what looked like a lone rider or a tree turned into a line of hard-riding cavalrymen galloping toward them. The four jumped on their horses and rushed to warn the Texas column. By the time the four men reached the column, it was already being surrounded by Mexican cavalry. Three of the four chose to escape and kept riding toward Victoria, 16 miles away. To his credit, Ehrenberg was the only one of the four to rejoin his encircled comrades.

Eight days later, Doctor Barnard accused the four horsemen of sleeping on duty, allowing the column to be surprised and surrounded.

Captain Shackelford described the event:

"We halted near an hour, then took up the march…. We had advanced about four miles, when a large force of cavalry were seen emerging from the timber, about two miles distant, and to the West of us. About one half of this force (350 men) were detached and thrown in front of our right flank, with the intention of cutting us off from a skirt of timber, about one mile and a half in front. Our artillery was ordered to open upon them and cover our rear."

Most of the Texans had never seen so many Mexican cavalrymen. Their estimates of the number varied from several hundred (Shackelford's) to a thousand.

Captain Horton's 50 man mounted advance guard was cut off from the column by the swift attack of Mexican cavalry. Seeing that the Mexicans had completely surrounded Fannin's main body, Horton's men rode away toward Victoria, despite orders and angry protests from Horton. Despairing, Horton followed his rangers away from the already encircled column.

Fannin and his men hoped that Horton and his company would momentarily break through the Mexican lines and reinforce them, perhaps even later, after darkness.

They were wrong. Horton and his troopers were well on their way to Victoria.

Horton's inability to reinforce Fannin at Coleto is analogous to Fannin's failure to reinforce Travis at the Alamo. Would either Coleto or the Alamo have resulted in a different outcome had those reinforcements arrived?

Hearing the enemy's firing, Fannin swore and jumped off his horse. "That's the signal for battle, I won't retreat another foot!" Reacting almost as swiftly as the enemy cavalry, Fannin curled his march column into a small sunken, rectangular defense position on the prairie. In West Point fashion, the corners of the square were laid out by compass.

One of the few survivors was Dr. Joseph E. Field who detailed the dismal scene:

"Our situation was very unfortunate, being in the midst of that large prairie, in a place where the ground was much lower than that around us. We were also without water, which is the greatest of necessities, especially for the wounded. The enemy having closed around us, upon every side, made a general charge but was repulsed with great slaughter. They rallied and charged again and again; but at every succeeding charge with less vigor, until night came and put an end to the carnage. The enemy retired to the woods in the direction of our march. When they had taken their position for the night, Col. Fanning ordered his men to prepare for resuming their march and cutting their way through the enemy's lines. But it was soon discovered, that so many of our horses were killed or wounded, and our oxen strayed away, that it was impossible to transport our wounded, who were more than sixty in number. Our commander said he would not leave them, but was resolved to share with them a common fate."

Fannin's decision to remain in the depressed square location rather than move into the woods during darkness resulted from yet another "consultation." D.H. Duval of the Kentucky Mustangs wrote "it was unanimously determined to not abandon our wounded men, but to remain with them and share their fate, whatever it might be."

Captain Shackelford also described their unfortunate defensive position:

"The prairie here was nearly in the form of a circle. In front was the timber of the Coleto, about a mile distant; in the rear was another strip of timber, about six miles distant; whist on our right and left, equidistant, four or five miles from us, there were, likewise bodies of timber. The order of battle was that of a hollow square. But unfortunately for us, in endeavoring to reach a commanding eminence in the prairie, our ammunition cart broke down, and we were compelled to take our position in a valley, six or seven feet below the mean base, of about one fourth of a mile in area. I have said that the order of battle was that of a hollow square; I should more properly say an oblong square.

"The Red Rovers and the New Orleans' Greys formed the front line of the square; the Red Rovers being on the extreme right. Colonel Fannin took a commanding position, directly in rear of the right flank. Our orders were not to fire until the enemy approached in point blank shot. The cavalry on our right dismounted, about 350 strong, and when within about a quarter mile of us, gave a volley with their *scopets* (shotguns), which came whizzing over our heads. They still continued to advance, and from the proximity of the second volley of balls over our heads, I ordered my company to sit down, which example was followed by all, excepting the artillerists."

Note: The New Orleans' Grays Shackelford described on his left flank were probably a mix of New Orleans, San Antonio and Mobile Greys.

Captain Shackelford continued. "The third volley from their pieces wounded the man on my left, and several others. About this time, Colonel Fannin had the cock of his rifle shot away by a ball, and another buried in the breech. He was still standing erect, a conspicuous mark, giving orders 'not to fire yet' in a calm and decided manner. The enemy had now advanced within about one hundred yards of us: they halted and manifested a determination to give us a regular battle. At this moment we opened our fire on them, rifles, muskets and artillery. Colonel Fannin, at the same time, received a severe wound in the fleshy part of the thigh, the bullet passing obliquely over the bone, carrying with it a part his pocket-handkerchief.

At this crisis, the enemy's infantry, from about ten to twelve hundred strong advanced on our left and rear."

Note: When his pocket handkerchief was pulled from Fannin's thigh wound, the musket slug came out with it.

Captain Shackelford continued his account. "Those on our left were the celebrated 'Tampico permanent Regiment,' of which Santa Anna said 'They are the best troops in the world.' When at a convenient distance, they gave us a volley and charged bayonet. So soon as the smoke cleared away, they were received by a piece of artillery, Duval's riflemen, and some other troops, which mowed them down with tremendous slaughter. Their career being thus promptly stopped, they contented themselves with falling down in the grass and occasionally raising up to fire; but whenever they showed their heads, they were taken down by the riflemen.

"The engagement now became general; and a body of cavalry, from one to two hundred strong, made a demonstration on our rear. "They came up in full tilt, with gleaming lances, shouting like Indians. When about sixty yards distant, the whole of the rear division of our little command, together with a piece or two of artillery, loaded with double canister filled with musket-balls, opened a tremendous fire upon them, which brought them to a full halt and swept them down by scores The rest immediately retreated, and chose to fight on foot the balance of the day. Our guns had now become hot—we had no water to sponge them—many of our artillerists had been wounded, and we had to rely alone on our small-arms…."

Shackelford's   detailed,   eye-witness,

company-commander account of Coleto details Urrea's willingness to sacrifice his soldiers. Not only was the severity of the battle detailed by Shackelford, so were the bravery and fortitude of the badly outnumbered, surrounded Texas defenders, operating without water or food. Casualties among the defenders were also mounting although at a slower rate than that of Urrea's soldiers.

Urrea's diary reports similar sacrifice and bravery. "Though our soldiers showed resolution, the enemy was likewise unflinching. Thus, without being intimidated by our impetuous charge, it maneuvered in order to meet it; and assuming a hammer formation on the right, they quickly placed three pieces of artillery on this side, pouring a deadly shower of shot upon my reduced column. A similar movement was executed on the left, while our front attack was met with the same courage and coolness. Our column was obliged to operate in guerillas in order to avoid, as far as possible, the withering fire of the enemy, who kept up a most lively fire, for each one of their soldiers had three and even four loaded guns which they could use at the most critical moment."

Urrea took special notice of Fannin's artillery since Urea had none himself at the moment. "The fire of the nine cannons, itself lively and well directed, was imposing enough; but our soldiers were brave to rashness and seemed to court death."

Ehrenberg of the Greys also remembered the effectiveness of the artillery that day:

"Our artillery officers, tall, fine-looking Poles, decided likewise to let the enemy's cavalry draw nearer before opening fire. Finally, when the Mexican horsemen had come close enough to us, our front line moved aside so as to leave free range to our cannon, which poured heavy shot upon our hasty and overconfident assailants.

"The effect of our artillery fire was immediate and horrible. Frightened by the noise, the horses of the enemy plunged and kicked wildly. Many of the Mexicans were thrown off their saddles, and their riderless horses galloped aimlessly across the field, while wounded men and beasts lying prostrate in the dust were trampled upon by the advancing or retreating cavalry squadrons."

Urrea's casualties were estimated at 50 killed and 140 wounded, but the numbers may be imprecise. At that point, the Mexicans were forced to retreat due to a lack of ammunition. Urrea admitted "I was forced to retire— not without indignation." De la Pena's report added, "The enemy seemed unaware of this, for he did not take advantage of a situation that was invaluable to him."

Urrea gathered his repulsed troops together for a review of the situation and pep talk:

"Our forces gathered in orderly fashion at the designated point of reunion. I joined them here and addressed them in terms suited to the occasion, but the troops needed no exhortations, for far from being discouraged at seeing their efforts frustrated, they were *burning with desire* (italics added) to undertake another bayonet charge. After so many hardships, a new attempt, besides being dangerous, was unadvisable. I concluded by saying to the soldiers just as the day closed: Let us gather our forces, let us wait for our ammunition and artillery, let us watch the enemy during the night and tomorrow I shall lead you to victory. You do not need your cartridges, for you have your bayonets, and your courage is boundless. The enemy is terrified and will not be able to resist any longer the charge of such brave Mexicans. I promise you a complete victory."

Shackelford's level-headed account of the battle continued:

"The action commenced about one o'clock, and continued, without intermission, until after sunset. Our whole force did not exceed two hundred and seventy effective men. That of the enemy (from all the information we could get) was reckoned at seven hundred Cavalry, and twelve hundred Infantry! Our loss was seven killed, besides several mortally wounded, and sixty badly wounded. We had many others slightly wounded. Out of the number killed, four belonged to my company; and more than one half of my company were struck with balls during the battle."

Meanwhile Houston received word from a courier that Fannin had been attacked a short distance from La Bahia. The details were unknown and would be for several days. Nonetheless, Houston berated Fannin for not earlier following his orders to abandon and destroy the fortress of La Bahia.

"If what I have heard from Fannin be true, I deplore it, and only attribute the ill luck to his attempting to retreat in daylight in the face of a superior force. He is an ill-fated man."

Houston's remark was prophetic.

A few days earlier Houston had reprimanded Fannin in writing. "You have received my orders, sir, repeatedly and have not obeyed them. My last directed you & your command to join the main army—a sufficient time elapsed for you to do so—the Special order was not obeyed. Your general conduct meets with my decided disapprobation."

Fannin was not the only target of Houston's wrath. He wrote Rusk, the Secretary of War, "For heaven's sake, do not drop again (move) with the seat of government! Your removal to Harrisburg has done more to increase the panic in the country than anything else that has occurred in Texas, except the fall of the Alamo."

Without Horton's horses to move his wounded to a wooded area—and establish a new defensive position within the timbers—Fannin had little option but remain in the crowded, small square. During the night, amidst Mexican bugle calls intimating further attacks, Fannin had men dig trenches and pile dead horses and baggage outside them for protection against the onslaught expected in the morning.

Doctor Barnard recollected the labors of that dark, dismal night:

"We went to work with our spades and dug a trench

three or four feet in depth. Our carts were then drawn up and disposed upon the breastworks so as to aid in our protection and the carcasses of two horses (all that we had along with us) and two or three oxen were piled up for bastions. Thus the night wore away, the enemy's patrol keeping up incessant music with their bugles to regale us, while the shrill and discordant scream of *Sentinel Alerto!* which afterwards became so familiar, then first jarred on my ear. I worked with the spade until fatigued, then lay down for a little troubled sleep, until the chillness of my limbs forced me to seek warmth by using the spade again, and in such alternations the dismal night was passed and day at last dawned on us."

Earlier the artillery ammunition was limited to only one or two rounds per cannon. The specially trained soldiers manning the cannon were in even shorter supply since they were prime targets for Mexican marksmen. Several of their bodies surrounded the cannon they formerly serviced.

Even rifle ammunition was scarce by evening. Musket ammunition was too large to be used in most of the volunteers' long rifles. Of all the scarcities, water was the most critical. There was none to dress wounds nor for the wounded to drink. The volunteers had been without water most of the grueling day, with no relief in sight.

Urrea planned one more charge of the small "oblong square" containing Fannin's trapped men. Mexican records dramatically described the action:

"As the fanfare sounded, which was the agreed signal, the forces advanced with great determination and bravery until they were within forty or fifty paces of the enemy's ranks. Their efforts were beyond description, the soldiers took the fire of the bullets from the rifles with breasts bared, and consequently the fire began to lessen notably, and their ammunition was being used up. Under such circumstances the general ordered the infantry to fix bayonets and maintain a slow fire. For better than half an hour both forces remained in this position until the general saw the impossibility of involving the enemy at that time and that the fight was unequal, and he gave the order to retreat."

In a classic understatement, Urrea claimed his losses that day were only "eleven killed, and forty-nine soldiers and five officers were wounded."

Doctor Barnard, later forced to tend the Mexican wounded, estimated that between three and four hundred were killed or wounded.

That evening Fannin suggested that an escape during the night would be better than waiting for a renewed and reinforced Mexican assault the next morning. He called for a vote on a possible breakout attempt which was rejected by the men. No one wanted to leave the wounded behind at the mercy of the Mexicans. Had Horton and his company returned to Coleto with reinforcements, the volunteers thought they might not only survive but possibly win a victory. Finding

Victoria abandoned, Horton pushed on to Gonzales to seek reinforcements. None were forthcoming.

Ehrenberg, always the alert observer, wrote about that fearsome night:

"The groans of the wounded increased the misery and horror of our situation. The cries of pain uttered by the stricken soldiers, the muffled thuds arising from the building of our barricades, and the challenges of the Mexican sentries broke the silence of the prairie, which lay dark and cheerless around us. There was not the smallest breath of air, and the moisture of the atmosphere added to the discomfort of our wounded companions. A few of them, consumed by burning fever... begged pitifully for water. Our canteens were empty, and although it wrung our hearts to see them suffer, we could not even moisten their parched lips with a drop of water."

That morning Urrea's soldiers feasted on hardtack and the freshly roasted meat from Fannin's slain oxen. There was no shortage of fresh water among the Mexican troops. In the crowded oblong square containing the trapped volunteers, many of them wounded, there was neither food nor water.

Shackelford continues his observations of the new day:

"The morning of the 20th came; but instead of a reinforcement, as we had anticipated, the reverse was the fact. The enemy had an accession to their remaining number of about five hundred men. Their whole force was then displayed in the most impossible and pompous manner; together with about three hundred pack mules keeping, however concealed, some pieces of artillery. These, being masked, were placed upon an elevated piece of ground, and were poured upon us; but without any effect. They took care to keep without the range of our rifles. Our cannon had become cool and we could have returned their fire; but perhaps with no effect and therefore reserved all for close quarters…"

CHAPTER 14

SURRENDER WITH DISCRETION...OR WAS IT?

There was no common consensus about surrendering. The soldiers themselves were not polled as they had been in the past. Dissent, particularly among the Red Rovers (despite Captain Shackelford's below assertion) and New Orleans' Greys, became threatening.

Herman Ehrenberg, one of the original New Orleans' Greys, remembered near mutiny among the Greys. (probably a mixture of San Antonio, Mobile and New Orleans'):

"After upbraiding Fannin for his weakness, they reminded him of the disastrous fate which had overtaken the other volunteers who sought safety in a truce with the treacherous Mexicans."

The Greys were in the minority and, eventually, all acceded and stacked their arms.

As the Mexicans collected the arms of the volunteers, Captain Horton, leading a group of about 40 armed citizens, appeared in a nearby timber line. The surprised Mexicans formed to meet this new threat and Horton quickly withdrew. Later he admitted the following, including his criticism of Fannin's surrender:

"But what fright took possession of us as we concluded the results of the fateful morning from the position of the Mexican troops! We stood in astonishment and were undecided (what) to do when suddenly the war-like bugle notes of the Mexicans sounded. No time was to be lost; quickly we had to counsel and just as quickly we were ready. If Fannin had so far forgotten his duty as to surrender we were obliged to save ourselves for the Republic. Now was the time when Texas needed our arms and our guns. All of our volunteers were now either taken prisoners or were murdered. Consequently we turned our horses and speedily galloped back to Victoria to unite with Houston's troops at Gonzales."

Captain/Doctor Shackelford's Recollection of the "Surrender"

"After they had fired a few rounds at us, they raised a white flag...we then had a consultation of officers, a majority of whom believed that we could not save our wounded without a capitulation; and *but one solitary man in ranks would have surrendered at discretion* (italics added). We then raised a white flag, which was responded to by the enemy.

Note: Both sides contended that the other was the first to raise a white flag.

"Major Wallace was then sent out together with one or two others who spoke the Mexican language. They shortly returned, and reported that the Mexican General could capitulate with the commanding officer only. Col. Fannin, although quite lame, then went out with the flag. When he was about to leave our lines, the emotions of my mind were intense, and I felt some anxiety to hear the determination of the men. I remarked to him that I would not oppose a surrender, provided we could obtain an honorable capitulation; one, on which he could rely: that if he could not obtain such—come back—our graves are already dug—let us be buried together. To these remarks the men responded in a firm and determined manner; and *the Colonel assured us, that he never would surrender on any other terms* (italics added). He returned a short time thereafter and communicated the substance of an agreement entered into by Gen. Urrea and himself. Col. Holsinger, a German and an engineer in the Mexican service, together with several other officers, then came into our lines to consummate the arrangement. The first words of Col. Holsinger uttered after a very polite bow, were: Well, Gentlemen, in eight days, liberty and home. The terms of the Capitulation were then written in both the English and Mexican languages, and read two or three times by officers who could speak and read both languages. The instruments which embodied the terms of the Capitulation as agreed on, were then signed and interchanged in the most formal and solemn manner; and were in substance, as follows:

"1st. That we should be received and treated as prisoners of war according to the usages of the most civilized nations.

2d, That private property should be respected and restored: that the side arms of the officers should be given up.

3d. That the men should be sent to Copano, and thence to the United States in eight days, or so soon thereafter as vessels could be procured to take them.

4th, That the officers should be paroled and returned to the United States in like manner."

Captain Shackelford continued. "I assert most positively, that this Capitulation was entered into without which a surrender never would have been made. I know that when Santa Anna as a prisoner (later) he flattered many into a belief, that no Capitulation was made; and those who were disposed to distrust the solemn asseverations of their unfortunate and much injured compatriots, in arms, and take the bare word of an unprincipled tyrant as blood-thirsty as ever foully disgraced the annals of civilization, are welcome to all the benefit of such confidence and credulity."

Doctor Field's Account of the "Surrender"

Field's recollection of the surrender agreement between Urrea and Fannin is recorded in Field's book "Three Years in Texas." (see Recommended Reading) He wrote "the articles of capitulation were soon agreed upon by the two commanders and committed to writing with the necessary signatures and formalities. The articles were, that in consideration of our surrendering (numbers added) 1. Our lives should be ensured, 2. Our personal property restored, and 3. That we were to be treated, in all respects, as prisoners of war are treated among enlightened nations.

"We also received a *verbal promise* (italics added) to be sent, in eight days, to the nearest port, to be transported to the United States."

General Urrea's Version of the "Surrender"

His diary indicates "One hundred infantry, two four-pounders (not a twelve pounder), and a howitzer were added to my force. I placed these as a battery about 160 paces from the enemy protected by the rifle companies. I ordered the rest of the infantry to form a column that was to advance along the left of our battery when it opened fire. As soon as we did this and began our movement as planned, the enemy, without answering our fire, raised a white flag. I immediately ordered the battery to cease firing and instructed Lieu. Col. Morales, Captain Juan Jose Holzinger and my aide…to approach the enemy and ascertain their purpose The first of these returned soon after, stating that they wished to capitulate. My reply restricted itself to stating that I could not accept any terms except an *unconditional surrender* (italics added). Messrs. Morales and Salas proceeded to tell this to the commissioners of the enemy who had already come out of their trenches. Several communications passed between us; and desirous of putting an end to the negotiations, I went over to the enemy's camp and explained to their leader the impossibility in which I found myself of granting other terms than an unconditional surrender as proposed, in view of the fact of which I refused to subscribe to the capitulation submitted consisting of three articles."

Urrea remembers meeting with Fannin with some clarity and defensiveness:

"Addressing myself to Fannin and his companions…I said conclusively 'If you gentlemen wish to *surrender at discretion* (italics added), the matter is ended, otherwise I shall return to my camp and resume the attack…' Had I been in a position to do so, I would have at least granted them their life…about 400 prisoners fell into the hands of our troops. There were ninety-seven wounded, Fannin and several other leaders among them."

Holzinger Answers Fannin's Question

After Urrea's ultimatum about continuing the attack, Fannin and staff spoke together, then Fannin asked Holzinger, "Do you believe that the Mexican Government will not attempt to take away our lives?" Holzinger replied that there could be no guarantees but that "not a single example could be adduced that the Mexican Government had ordered a man to be shot who had trusted to their clemency."

Fannin paused before admitting, "I have no water; my wounded need attendance, I particularly recommend to you those unfortunate men and will deliver myself up to the discretion of the Mexican Government."

Urrea then ordered two copies of the surrender documents be prepared, one in English, the other in Spanish. The completed English version was to be handed to Fannin and the Spanish to Urrea. Signing both the completed documents were Urrea, Morales, Holzinger, Fannin and Wallace.

Fannin gathered his officers together to advise them of the terms which he enumerated: treatment as prisoners of war, respect of private property and to be sent to the United States after eight days. All of the officers agreed to these terms except Captain Burr H. Duval of the Kentucky Mustangs.

Duval accused Fannin as follows: "Sir! You have not only signed your death warrant, but the death warrants of all of us."

What Happened to the Two "Surrender" Documents?

The English language document probably was handed to Fannin who may have pocketed it. Subsequently, it was lost.

The Spanish document retained by Urrea was vague in comparison to the above recollections of Shackelford, Field and even Urrea. Apparently written by Wallace and Chadwick and translated into Spanish, this strange little "document" read as follows:

Article 1: The Mexican troops having placed their battery at a distance of one hundred and seventy paces from us and the firing having been renewed, we raised a white flag. Colonels Juan Morales, Colonel Mariano Salas and Lieutenant Colonel Juan Jose Holzinger of Engineers came immediately. We proposed to them to *surrender at discretion* (italics added) and they agreed.

Article 2: The commandant Fannin and the wounded shall be treated with all possible consideration possible upon the surrender of all their arms.

Article 3: The whole detachment shall be treated as prisoners of war and shall be subject to the *disposition of the Supreme Government* (italics added).

Camp on the Coleto between
Guadalupe and La Bahia
March 20, 1836

B.C. Wallace, commandant

J.M. Chadwick, Aide, Approved, James W. Fannin

If the above is accurate, there was no Mexican guarantee of the prisoners' lives, as Fannin told the men, nor a guarantee to restore personal property. No mention is made of the promised transportation via Copano within eight days, and return to the U.S.

Was Fannin deceived or the deceiver?

Some historians refer to an unstated but commonly accepted understanding that Geneal Urrea would intercede with Santa Anna on the behalf of the Texas prisoners. The "understanding" was that the Texans would be treated as prisoners of war and ultimately freed in the United States. This "understanding" is omitted from the above surrender document.

There is a further mystery to the above. To the Spanish-language surrender document, General Urrea later added a personal insurance clause:

"Since the white flag was raised by the enemy, I made it known to their officer that I could not grant any other terms than unconditional surrender and they agreed to it through the officers expressed, those who subscribe the surrender have no right to any other terms. They have been informed of this fact and they are agreed. I ought not, cannot, nor wish to grant any other terms."

Monument on the Coleto Battlefield
Where Fannin Surrendered
(Photo courtesy NK Rogers)

CHAPTER 15
_____

RETURN TO LA BAHIA AS
PRISONERS OF WAR

Less than one hour after surrendering, some 240 men who had marched out of La Bahia the day before to fight were now marched back—but as prisoners heavily guarded by about 200 Mexicans. They would be imprisoned in their former fortress home whose defenses they had labored long and hard to improve. They must have thought their labors particularly useless as they were all crammed into the small chapel whose scant dimensions were about 30 by 85 feet.

For three days they were kept there without food—and very little water—penned like cattle. Approximately 240 men, many of them wounded, were crowded into 2550 square feet of space, which equates to about 10.6 square feet per individual. The Mexican guards demanded an open path through the prisoners, thus considerably reducing the space available per individual.

Ehrenberg wrote about the tiny chapel's overcrowding: "Several of my companions were so exhausted that they slept standing up, for the crowded state of the prison prevented us from laying down. A few of our smaller companions who could sit down enjoyed greater repose than the others. But even then they could not remain in their sitting position very long, for the atmosphere grew so close that squatting on the floor was bearable for a short time only."

To deter escape, the Mexicans positioned a loaded cannon in front of the chapel door and "the Mexicans who stood by held lighted wicks in their hands....I firmly believe," Ehrenberg continued, "that the enemy's plan was to starve us into rebellion and then to massacre us when we tried to secure our rights by force. Such conduct would have given a very plausible excuse to Santa Anna and his colleagues for our deaths."

Colonel Holzinger called together all of those prisoners who came from Germany and offered them their freedom if they would join the Mexican Army after abandoning the Texans. They indignantly rejected the offer, according to Ehrenberg. He added a memorable allegiance:

"Nothing stood between us now. We were no longer English, German, or Americans; we were Texans."

"After our arms had been given up (Shackelford's account continued) mid the necessary arrangements made, all who not so badly wounded as to prevent their marching, were posted off to Goliad under a strong guard. We reached there a little after sunset, and were driven into the church like so many swine. We were compelled to keep a space open in the centre for the guard to pass backward and forward, and under the penalty of having it kept open by a discharge of guns. To avoid this, we had literally to lie one upon another. Early in the morning, their soldiery commenced drawing blankets from our wounded. I resisted an attempt of this sort near me, and had a bayonet drawn and thrust at me.

"So soon as it was sufficiently light to see well, I commenced (with what little means I could procure), dressing and attending our wounded; but I was soon summoned by some Mexican officers, who came to the church door, to attend them. From that moment I found I had to labor in the hospital, and that scarcely an hour in the day would be allowed me to attend to my wounded companions. On the second day after our arrival, Col. Fannin and the wounded who were left behind arrived at the Fort; the men having scarcely any water, being compelled to bring it from the river in canteens; nor had we any other food than a scanty pittance of beef without bread or salt. Col. Fannin was then under the protection of Colonel Holzinger. On passing from one part of their wounded to another, I made it convenient to see Fannin, and stated to him how badly we were boarded. He immediately wrote to Gen. Urrea, adverting to the terms of the Capitulation, and to our treatment. He told me a promise was given him, that every comfort in their power should be provided for us in future.

"Let me here ask, if there had been no Capitulation, why did not Gen. Urrea advert to the fact, when Col.

Fannin urged upon him the immediate observance of its requirements?

"The next day Col. Fannin went in company with Col. Holzinger, on their way to Copano for the purpose of chartering a vessel, then said to be there, to take himself and men to the United States. When they reached that place, however, the vessel had departed. This, I afterwards learned, was a stratagem to get possession of one of the vessels belonging to Uncle Sam's folks; thinking the old fellow too good-natured to resist any little breach of that kind. On the 23d, Major Miller and about seventy men were brought in, having been taken at Copano on the 25th, Col. Ward and command, taken, as I before said, near Victoria."

Miller and his men of the Nashville Battalion had just arrived aboard the schooner *William and Frances*. They were unarmed, bathing on the beach after their voyage from New Orleans when Urrea's cavalry easily captured them.

Was the promise of being shipping home from Copano on the *William and Frances* simply a ruse intended to discourage prisoners from attempting escape?

After three days of captivity in the tiny chapel, the unwounded prisoners were transferred to an area along the west wall of the fortress. The 55 or so wounded remained in the chapel.

That day, March 23, Doctor Barnard recorded the following:

"My first effort was to see Col. Fannin, and if, by any possibility through him get hold of some of our surgical instruments and hospital dressings for the wounded, we having been robbed of everything of the kind. Much of said articles had belonged to individuals, and Col. Fannin, at my request, addressed a note to the Mexican commandant, in which he claimed sundry instruments and other articles, not only as personal property according to the terms of the Capitulation, but from the necessity of the surgeons having them for the benefit of the wounded Mexicans as well as of the Americans. The application was of no avail, and I should not mention it except to show that the terms of the capitulation had been appealed to once by Col. Fannin, which, of course, he never would have done had there been no capitulation."

Return of Fannin from Copano

"Our treatment did not vary much during the week," Shackelford maintained, "except that the men were marched into an area of the Fort, without any protection or covering; and the Church filled with a part of their wounded; ours occupying the barracks, or rather one small room. On the 26th, Col. Fannin returned. That night I slept in a small room with him and some other officers. This room was in one corner of the Church, and was where we kept our medicines, instruments, bandages, & c. Col. Fannin was quite cheerful, and we talked pleasantly of the prospect of our reaching the United States. I cannot, bore, resist an inclination to mention one more incident of that evening—the last evening of many very gallant spirits. It had a peculiar effect upon my feelings, and never can be erased from the tablet of my memory."

Their Last Evening

Shackelford pensively recalled the night of March 26. "Many of our young men had a fondness for music, and could perform well, particularly on the flute. In passing by them to visit some wounded, on the outside of the Fort, my ear caught the sound of music, as it rolled in harmonious numbers from several flutes in concert. The tune was 'Home, Sweet Home.' I stopped for a few moments and gazed upon my companions with an intense and painful interest. As these 'notes of mournful touch' stole upon the breeze, the big tear that rolled down many a manly cheek, which had glowed in battle and burned in the rage of conflict, told the heart's irrepressible emotion; for the image of home and friends came over the mind 'like the pressure of a spirit-hand.'

"Poor fellows! It was their last earthly evening. Little did they then dream, that the next morning, Treachery would consign them to their everlasting home! Subsequent events rendered it easier for me to forget all the scenes of a thousand days of pleasurable enjoyment, than to cease to remember this one incident ofthose few lonely minutes of grief."

CHAPTER 16

APOLOGIA

U rrea knew exactly what Santa Anna's intentions were for the prisoners of war locked up in La Bahia. With an eye to his future reputation, Urrea distanced himself from the coming massacre by riding off to Victoria in pursuit of Captain Horton and his few horsemen. Urrea left a lieutenant colonel in charge of the almost 400 prisoners, awaiting the murderous order shortly expected from Santa Anna. Urrea wouldn't be present, thus exonerating himself of what was certainly to follow.

Urrea's diary reads:

"On the 27th, between nine and ten in the morning, I received a communication from Lieut. Col. Portilla, military commandant at that point, telling me that he had received orders from His Excellency, the general-in-chief, to shoot all the prisoners and that he was making preparations to fulfill that order.

"This order was received by Portilla at seven in the evening of the 26th, and although he notified me of the fact that same date, his communication did not reach me until after the execution had been carried out. All the members of my division were distressed to hear this news, and I no less, being as sensitive as my companions who will bear testimony of my excessive grief. Let a single one of them deny this fact! More than 150 prisoners who were with me escaped this terrible fate; also those who surrendered at Copano and the surgeons and hospital attendants were spared.

"…There have not been lacking those who would hold me responsible, although my conduct in the affair was straightforward and unequivocal. The orders of the general-in-chief with regard to the fate decreed for prisoners was very emphatic. "These orders always seemed to me harsh, but they were the inevitable result of the barbarous and inhuman decree which declared outlaws those whom it wanted to convert into citizens of the republic….I wished to elude these orders as far as possible without compromising my personal responsibility; and, with this object view, I issued orders to Lieut. Col. Portilla, instructing him to use the prisoners for the rebuilding of Goliad."

Note: Despite his above order about rebuilding La Bahia with POW labor, Urrea had not left Portilla enough soldiers to adequately guard prisoners laboring in several locations.

Urrea's lengthy self defense continued:
"…I never thought that the horrible spectacle of that

massacre could take place in cold blood… It was painful for me, also, that so many brave men should thus be sacrificed, particularly the much esteemed and fearless Fannin. They doubtlessly surrendered confident that Mexican generosity would not make their surrender useless, for under any other circumstances they would have sold their lives dearly, fighting to the last. I had due regard for the motives that induced them to surrender, and for this reason I used my influence with the general-in-chief to save them, if possible, from being *butchered* (italics added), particularly Fannin. I obtained from His Excellency a severe reply, repeating his previous order, *doubtlessly dictated by cruel necessity* (italics added). Fearing, no doubt, that I might compromise him with my disobedience and expose him to the accusations of his enemies, he transmitted his instructions directly to the commandant at Goliad, inserting a copy of the order to me.

"…While that tragic scene was being enacted in Goliad I was in Guadalupe Victoria, where I received word of it several hours after the execution, what could I do to prevent it, specially if the orders were transmitted directly to that place?

"This is to demand the impossible, and had I been in a position to disregard the order it would have been a violent act of insubordination. If they wish to argue that it was in my hand to have guaranteed the lives of those unfortunates by granting them a capitulation when they surrendered at Perdido (Coleto), I will reply that it was not in my power to do it, nor it was not honorable, either to arms of the nation or to myself, to have done so. Had I granted them terms, I would then have laid myself open to a trial…I could not admit any proposals except a surrender at discretion, my duty being to continue fighting, leaving the outcome to fate. I believe that I acted in accordance with my duty and that I could not do otherwise. Those who assert that I offered guarantees to those who surrendered, speak without knowledge of the facts."

Throughout his South Texas campaign, Urrea played a duplicitous game with Santa Anna, benefiting many prisoners. At times he complied with the order to shoot the prisoners, e.g., Captain Amon King and 14 of his captured men were shot at Refugio.

At other times, Urrea relented—heeding the pleas of Father Thomas J. Malloy, Senora Alavez or others—sending some of the prisoners taken at San Patricio and Agua Dulce to prison in Matamoros. Urrea then apologized to Santa Anna for his failure to obey the "shoot the pirates" decree of December 10.

Urrea wrote Lt. Col. Portilla, whom he had left in charge of the Goliad prisoners, to use the POWs to rebuild Goliad. Faced with conflicting orders from Santa Anna (shoot the POWs) and Urrea (use them to rebuild), Urrea well knew which order Portilla would follow.

Here is a portion of Santa Anna's letter to Portilla:

"I am informed that there has been sent to you by General Urrea two hundred and forty prisoners…. As the supreme government has ordered all foreigners taken with arms in their hands, making war upon the nation, shall be treated as pirates. I have been surprised that the circular of said government has not been fully complied with in this particular. I therefore order that you should give immediate effect to the said ordnance in respect to all those foreigners who have yielded to the force of arms, having had the audacity to come and insult the republic, to devastate with fire and sword, as has been the case in Goliad, causing vast detriment to our citizens, in a word, shedding the precious blood of Mexican citizens, whose only crime had been their fidelity to their country. I trust that, in reply to this, you will inform me that public vengeance has been satisfied by the punishment of such detestable delinquents."

Santa Anna was not hesitant to later plead his own case:

"Law commands," he wrote, "and the magistrate has no power to mitigate its rigor; for him it is to put it into execution. If, in the execution of law, no discretion is allowed a judge, how can a general in a campaign be expected to exercise greater freedom?"

De la Pena, careful observer and critic of his general-in-chief, remembered there was "general outrage in the army regarding the criminal immorality of the exterminations." He specifically decried Portilla's "crimes against humanity" and especially their occurrence on Palm Sunday.

Later captured at San Jacinto, Santa Anna claimed he had *not* ordered the execution of the prisoners. He blamed Urrea for the murders. Santa Anna went so far to prove his innocence, that he claimed he would execute Urrea for accepting the surrender of Fannin and his men.

White Door of the Chapel where the Prisoners
Unknowingly Awaited Massacre
Photo courtesy NK Rogers

CHAPTER 17

MASSACRE MORNING, PALM SUNDAY, MARCH 27

*"As we passed a door an officer told
me we all were to be shot."*
Andrew Michael Boyle, Westover's Company

The weather that Palm Sunday, March 27, was humid, overcast and oppressive, a bellwether of what was to follow that terrible morning.

Lieutenant Colonel Jose Nicolas de la Portilla, in charge of the fort and prisoners during Urrea's carefully planned absence, kept a diary of that terrible event:

"March 26. At seven in the evening I received orders from General Santa Anna by special messenger, instructing me to execute at once all prisoners taken by force of arms agreeable to the general orders on the subject. (I have the original order in my possession.) I kept the matter secret and no one knew of it except Col.

Garay, to whom I communicated the order. At eight o'clock, on the same night, I received a communication from Gen. Urrea by special messenger in which among other things he says, *"Treat the prisoners well, especially Fannin. Keep them busy rebuilding the town and erecting a fort. Feed them with the cattle you will receive from Refugio."* What a cruel contrast in these opposite instructions! I spent a restless night.

"March 27. At daybreak, I decided to carry out the orders of the general-in-chief because I considered them superior. I assembled the whole garrison and ordered the prisoners, who were still sleeping, to be awakened. There were 445. (The eighty that had just been taken at Copano and had, consequently, not borne arms against the government, were set aside) The prisoners were divided into three groups and each was placed in charge of an adequate guard, the first under Augustin Alcerrica, the second under Capt. Luis Balderas, and the third under Capt. Antonio Ramirez. I gave orders to these officers to carry out the orders of the supreme government and the general-in-chief. This was immediately done. There was a great contrast in the feelings of the officers and the men. Silence prevailed. Sad at heart I wrote to Gen. Urrea expressing my regret at having been concerned in so painful an affair. I also sent an official account of what I had done, to the general-in-chief."

One of the Red Rovers, Dillard C. Cooper, was among the prisoners awakened that morning. The prisoners believed they were being marched off to

Copano Bay to board transport to the United States. Another story circulating among them was that they were hunting stray cattle. Cooper and his group filed into a hollow square lined with armed soldiers. There they were formed into two files and headed southwest. There were two guards per every prisoner in Cooper's group of Red Rovers and Westover Regulars.

Note: Several prisoners wondered why their guards were wearing their parade uniforms, instead of the normal duty uniform. They must have thought to themselves, "What's the occasion?"

After a few minutes Cooper's group was halted parallel to a brush fence. Their guards reassembled on one side, about eight feet from the prisoners who were ordered to face the fence, i.e., away from the guards. Realizing what was happening, prisoners began pleading for their lives. Alabaman Robert Fenner called out, "Don't take on so, boys; if we have to die, let's die like brave men."

Dillard Cooper was among the fortunate four Red Rovers managing to escape their executioners that day.

John Duval, a surviving Kentucky Mustang, was herded out the fort's south gate toward the northwest. Here is his recollection:

"When about a mile above town (Goliad), a halt was made and the guard on the side next to the river filed around to the opposite side. Hardy had this maneuver been executed, when I heard a heavy firing of musketry in the directions taken by the other two divisions. Someone near me exclaimed, 'Boys! They are about to shoot us!' and at the same instant I heard the clicking of musket locks all along the Mexican line. I turned to look, and as I did so, the Mexicans fired upon us, killing probably one hundred out of one hundred fifty men in the division."

Sketch of Coleto Battlefield and the Three
Massacre Sites outside La Bahia
(Photo courtesy NK Rogers)

Captain Jack Shackelford also remembered that dreadful Palm Sunday morning:

"Never…can I forget the horrors of this fatal morning. At dawn we were awakened by a Mexican officer calling us up and saying, he 'wanted the men to form a line, that they may be counted.' On hearing this, my impression was, that in all probability some poor fellows had made their escape during the night. After leaving the Church, I was met by Colonel Guerrear (Garay), said to be the Adjutant General of the Mexican Army. This officer spoke the English language as fluently as I did myself; and to his honour be it said, he seemed a gentleman and a man of feeling. He requested that I go to his tent in company of Major Miller and men; and that I would take my friend and companion, Joseph Bernard (Dr. James H. Barnard) with me. We accordingly went over to his tent, about one hundred yards off, in a south-easterly direction. On passing the gate of the Fort, I saw Ward's men in line, with their knapsacks on. I inquired of them where they were going, some of them stated that they were to march to Copano, and from thence to be sent home! After reaching Colonel Guerrear's tent (to attend some wounded, as we expected,) we sat down and engaged in familiar conversation with a little Mexican officer who had been educated in Bardstown, Ky. In about half an hour, we heard the report of a volley of small arms, towards the river, and to the east of the Fort. I immediately inquired the cause of the firing; and was assured by the officer that he 'did not know, but expected it was the guard firing off their guns.' In about fifteen or twenty minutes thereafter, another such volley was fired, directly south of us, and in front. At the same time, I could distinguish the heads of some men through the boughs of some peach trees, and could hear their screams. It was then, for the first time, the awful conviction seized upon our minds that Treachery and Murder had begun their work. Shortly afterwards, Col. Guerrear (Garay) appeared at the mouth of the tent."

Colonel Garay said to the physicians "Keep still, gentlemen, you are safe; these are not my orders, nor do I execute them."

Shackelford asked Garay "if it could be possible they were murdering our men? He replied that it was so but that he had done all in his power to save as many as he could; and that if he could have saved more, he would have done so."

Doctors Barnard and Shackelford sat next to each other in Garay's tent while the musketry continued to boom outside. Shackelford, Barnard reported, was in agony. "His company of 'Red Rovers' that he brought out and commanded were young men of the first families in his neighborhood—his particular and esteemed friends. Besides, two of his nephews who had volunteered with him, and his eldest son, a talented youth, the pride of his father and beloved of his company, were there." From the sounds of the Mexican musket volleys, he knew his kin were being slaughtered but could do nothing except sit and endure.

Shackelford wrote, "The men were taken out in four divisions, and under different pretexts; such as making room in the Fort for the reception of Santa Anna, going-out to slaughter beef, and being marched off to Copano, to be sent home. In about an hour, the closing scene this base and treacherous tragedy was acted in the Fort and the cold-blooded murder of all the wounded, who were unable to be marched out, was its infernal catastrophe."

Note: Captain Shackelford mentioned four divisions, probably counting the wounded who were slaughtered outside the chapel as a division. The Georgia Battalion and Kentucky Mustangs were marched to an area northwest of La Bahia and slaughtered there. The Red Rovers and Westover's Regulars were massacred at a site southwest of La Bahia. The third site, where the New Orleans, Mobile and other Greys were murdered, was northeast of La Bahia.

There were a few survivors of the massacre, Herman Ehrenberg of the Greys among them. Luckily he was not hit in the initial discharge of muskets due to the smoke, noise and confusion. He was able to dive to the ground, then sprint toward the San Antonio River. One Mexican tried to plunge his sword into him but Ehrenberg avoided the thrust and dived into the river. On the other side, he paused, caught his breath and turned. "I looked back at the place where my friends lay bleeding to death. The enemy was still shooting and yelling, and it was with a sorrowful heart that I listened to these shouts of triumph which in my fancy were mingled with the groans of pain of my dying friends."

"I learned from the interpreter (Spohn)," Shackelford wrote, "that Col. Fannin was the last doomed captive of vengeance; that he was ordered to communicate the fact to him."

The last English words the 31 year-old Fannin

heard were from interpreter Joseph Spohn, ordered to translate for Fannin the following:

"That for having come with an armed band to commit depredations and revolutionize Texas, the Mexican Government were about to *chastise* him." (italics added)

Note: One version of the execution is that Fannin fixed his own blindfold. Another version has Spohn doing it, yet another, Mexican Captain Huerta.

Fannin asked Spohn to make one last request of the Mexican captain: "…tell them not to place their muskets so near as to scorch his face with the powder." The officer standing behind them, after seeing their muskets were brought within two feet of his body, drew forth his handkerchief as a signal, when they fired, and poor Fannin fell dead on the right side of the chair, and from thence rolled into a dry ditch, about three feet deep, close by the wall."

Shackelford continued, "Fannin met his fate in a calm and soldier-like manner; that he handed his watch to the officer who superintended his murder, with it request that he would have him decently interred; and that he should be shot in the breast, and not in the head; with all of which the officer solemnly promised to comply; that Fannin was then placed in a chair, tied the handkerchief over his eyes with his own hands, then opened his bosom to receive their balls. Major Miller, who knew Fannin, informed me that the next day he saw him lying in the prairie among a group of wounded; and that he was shot in the head!"

Note: The Mexican officer in charge of Fannin's murder detail was Captain Carolino Huerta of the Tres Villas Battalion. Fannin handed him the letter he'd just written his wife plus his watch and some coins. Huerta's soldiers removed the bayonets from their muskets, then, at their captain's command, fired at Fannin's head from about two feet away.

Where Fannin was Executed in a Chair in
a Northwest Corner of La Bahia
Photo courtesy NK Rogers

"We were marched into the Fort about 11 o'clock," Shackelford continued his sorrowful account, "and ordered to the Hospital. Had to pass close by our butchered companions, who were stripped of their clothes and their naked, mangled bodies thrown in a pile. The wounded were all hauled out in carts that evening; and some brush thrown over the different piles, with a view of burning, their bodies. A few days afterwards, I accomplished Major Miller to the spot where lay those who were dear to me whilst living; and whose memory will be embalmed in my affection…The flesh had been burned from off the bodies; but many hands and feet were yet unscathed—I could recognize no one. The bones were all still knit together, and the vultures were feeding upon those limbs which, one week before, actively played in battle."

Their bodies, including Fannin's, were dragged outside about a quarter of a mile from La Bahia and thrown into a pile.

Many Mexican officers, including Lieutenant Colonel de la Pena, may have been horrified by the butchery of prisoners of war at the Alamo and Goliad, but none attempted to intercede. The exception was Colonel Francisco Garay who told Shackelford he had saved as many prisoners as he could at Goliad and elsewhere. Doctors Shackelford and Barnard were among those whom Garay saved.

At San Patricio, Senora Francisca Alavez (or Alvarez) interceded with Urrea not to execute the prisoners taken there. Reuben R. Brown of Dr. Grant's command owed his life to this lady. "I was taken out to be shot but was spared through the intercession of a priest and a Mexican lady named Alvarez."

Dr. Barnard further described Senora Alvarez's action. "And when, on the morning of the massacre she learned the prisoners were to be shot, she so effectually pleaded with Colonel Garay (whose human feelings so revolted) that with great personal responsibility to himself, and at great hazards at thus going contrary to the orders of the then all-powerful Santa Anna, resolved to save all that he could; and a few of us, in consequence, were left to tell of that bloody day."

When she saw Captain Shackelford a few days later, she cried, "Why did I not know you had a son here? I would have saved him at all hazards."

A statue honoring Senora Alvarez, "The Angel of Goliad," was erected near La Bahia.

The Angel of Goliad: This statue just outside Presidio La Bahia honors the memory of Senora Francisca Alvarez (or Alavez). This heroic and compassionate lady saved countless prisoners from execution by the Mexican Army. Photo courtesy NK Rogers

How Many Prisoners Were Murdered that Day at Goliad/La Bahia?

Portilla, the acting commander in the absence of General Urrea, said there were 455 prisoners that morning. Most accounts agree 28 prisoners escaped slaughter. If true, there were 417 men mercilessly shot, bayoneted or beaten to death by the officers and soldiers of the Yucatan and Tres Villas battalions.

Historian Clarence Wharton wrote the following in "Remember Goliad":

"Three hundred and ninety men were killed in the Palm Sunday massacre at Goliad and twenty-seven escaped by running and evading hunters. Twenty-nine were spared for various reasons."

T.R. Fehrenbach's work, "Lone Star," agreed: 390 men were murdered.

Kathryn S. O'Connor, in her history of La Bahia lists the names of 352 men executed that Sunday.

J.H. Brown's "History of Texas" claims 390 men were massacred

The "Handbook of Texas" indicates 342 were executed at Goliad.

The Fannin monument outside La Bahia lists 353 names of the men massacred that Palm Sunday.

Several studies of man-for-man records of the carnage at La Bahia indicate a total of 342 prisoners were murdered. Twenty-eight others managed to escape. Major Miller's unarmed 80 men, captured on the beach at Copano, were spared. Twenty-six men from Lt. Colonel Ward's Georgia Battalion were not shot at Victoria because Colonel Holzinger wanted them used as carpenters. Colonel Garay's intervention was responsible for sparing the lives of Doctors Barnard, Field and Shackleford, plus their assistant, George Voss, and interpreter Joseph Spohn.

Other reports estimate the total between 428 and 445.

The exact number may never be known.

What Happened to the Absent General Urrea?

After Goliad, Urrea joined Santa Anna's attempt to corner Houston's ragged army, which it eventually and unsuccessfully did at San Jacinto. The never-defeated Urrea was enraged not only by Santa Anna's defeat by Houston's small command. He was also angered by Santa Anna's order to the Mexican Army to retreat back into Mexico.

Urrea's anger was not reserved for the vanquished Santa Anna. General Filisola's execution of Santa Anna's order to retreat from Texas gained Urrea's special ire. He wanted the pursuit of Houston continued, Houston cornered in East Texas and defeated. Most likely any prisoners taken there would have received the same fate as those at La Bahia.

General Filisola's description of the two Urrea victories at San Patricio and Refugio as "skirmishes" further enraged Urrea. Filisola charged that Urrea deserved trial by a "council of war" and punished for sacrificing "hundreds of brave soldiers when similar results could have been obtained, without such a sacrifice."

Urrea contrasts Filisola's above charge with the latter's letter to Urrea of April 20 in which Filisola described the same "skirmishes":

"I congratulate you for the brilliancy of your glorious operations, which, in my opinion, leave nothing to be desired."

Urrea accused another of his brother generals, Ganoa, of trading supplies intended for the army, monopolizing them, and "selling them to his brigade at a profit of more than a hundred percent."

Ganoa, Urrea added, "pillaged the town of Bastrop and delayed the march of the division for eight days in order to transport the booty."

If the Mexican Army was not demoralized during 1836, its quarreling general officers appear to have been.

In 1837, Urrea was named the commandant general of the two departments (states) of Sinaloa and Sonora. Disappointed, that he was passed over for promotion to governor, he quickly resolved the issue by federalizing the two departments. This allowed his appointment as the constitutional governor.

Still a soldier, he turned over his duties as constitutional governor to the vice governor and led a campaign against centralist forces in Mazatlan but was defeated.

He escaped and fled to the cities of Guaymas, then Durango. Again he became active in opposing the central government. In 1839 Urrea was captured and sent to Perote Prison in Vera Cruz.

Not done yet, his supporters rescued him from a Durango prison to lead them in another revolt. Successful this time, he was appointed governor of Sonora in 1842-1844. He was called to duty during the U.S.-Mexican War of 1846 and died three years later in 1849.

CHAPTER 18

TAPS

The bodies of the 390 victims were searched for valuables, stripped and piled together like rubbish. Half-hearted attempts to burn the remains were made.

On a Friday morning, June 3, the Texas Army led by Colonel Sidney Sherman was paraded before a large crowd of mourners near Goliad. The remains of the murdered men had been gathered and interred immediately outside the walls of Presidio La Bahia. Texas Secretary of War General Thomas J. Rusk delivered the eulogy, a portion of which follows:

"Fellow soldiers: In the order of Providence we are this day called upon the last offices of respect to the remains of the noble and heroic band who, battling for our sacred rights, have fallen beneath the ruthless hand of a tyrant. Relinquishing the ease, the peace and the comfort of their homes, leaving behind them all they held dear—their mothers, sisters, daughters and wives—they subjected themselves to fatigue and privation, and notably threw themselves between the people of Texas and the legions of Santa Anna...."

Among the mourners seated in front of General Rusk at that ceremony was Captain/Doctor Jack Shackelford, sorrowfully remembering his murdered eldest son and two nephews who rested there.

Shackelford relates the following about the last moment of two young volunteers as they heard the click of Mexican muskets behind them on that terrible Palm Sunday morning. Flourishing their caps over their heads, they shouted as loudly as possible "Hurra for Texas!" as they were shot dead.

A View of Fannin, Texas, population 125
(Photo Courtesy NK Rogers)

THE FIVE SPANISH MISSIONS

The Alamo (1718) (Mission San Antonio de Bexar)

The best know is the Alamo, where Travis and his 185-200 men were besieged by Santa Anna's 1800. Despite the odds, the defenders held out for thirteen days until the Mexicans' final, successful onslaught of March 6, 1836. Travis and his entire command were either killed during the battle or immediately executed.

The Alamo was established in 1718 as a way station between missions in East Texas and Mexico. It was already one hundred years old at the time of the historic battle for which the Alamo and Texas are famous.

Espada (1731) (Mission San Francisco de la Espada)

This mission was the temporary headquarters of General Stephen F. Austin, who successfully defeated Mexican General Cos and his force, driving them from Texas. Espada was the starting point from which Jim Bowie began his search for the best mission to serve as General Austin's base of operations against the Mexicans within the town.

San Juan (1731) (Mission San Juan de Capistrano)

This was the first mission examined by Jim Bowie and his ninety-two man force as a feasible operating base for General Austin's Texas Army. Concluding Espada was not easily defendable, Bowie continued up the San Antonio River to the next candidate mission.

Upon its founding in 1731, San Juan became the supply point for cattle, sheep and other agricultural products made by local Indians in its workshops.

San Jose (1720) (Mission San Jose y San Miguel de Aguayo)

Bowie and his scouts went there after examining San Juan and deemed it unsuitable as Austin's base of operations.

Five miles downstream from the Alamo, San Jose was built two years later. It became the area's social and cultural center and also housed the area's largest military garrison to defend the town against Indian attack.

Concepcion (1731) (Nuestra Senora de la Purisima Concepcion de Acuna)

Arriving at the last mission, Bowie found it the most suitable of all the others. Located near a bend of the San Antonio River, the location was easily defended and offered clear fields of fire against the enemy attack expected momentarily.

The most attractive of the missions, Concepcion has served as a center of religious activities and celebrations. Inside the mission are several well-preserved original religious paintings.

THE THREE SURGEONS

Three surgeons, in the midst of intense cruelty and suffering during the Texas Revolution, performed their medical duties to the fullest, including care of casualties on both sides.

Doctors Jack Shackelford, James E. Field and James H. Barnard came from differing and diverse backgrounds, giving up private practices to support the Texas revolution.

Their medical skills and compassion allowed their eventual escape from Mexican captivity. They were keen, first-hand, eye-witness observers of the chaos about them. Later each would record his harrowing experiences on the battlefield as well as in the hospital. All three were important chroniclers of this period of great historical consequence.

Dr. Shackelford was born in Richmond, Virginia, in 1790. A physician and surgeon, he moved to Winnsboro, North Carolina, in 1811 and married Maria Young. During the War of 1812, he served on the staff of General Andrew Jackson. Thereafter he moved again, to Shelby County, Alabama, and became a plantation owner as well as a state senator. His hometown was Courtland.

Heeding Sam Houston's appeal for assistance, Shackelford organized a company of volunteers dubbed the Alabama Red Rovers due to their red uniform trousers made by their wives and sweethearts and the solid red flag they carried.

Unlike his fellow physicians, Shackelford's initial primary duty was to command of a large volunteer rifle company. Additionally, he tended the medical problems inherent in a combat unit.

Shackelford and Barnard were particular friends, having met as the Red Rovers reached the Texas coast. At the end, the two surgeons/friends parted at Velasco, having ridden together for three months following the Goliad/Coleto scenes of death and mutilation.

His acute memories of the war in Texas are detailed in "Captain Jack Shackelford's Account of the Goliad Massacre." (see Recommended Reading) Fifty two Red Rovers were killed in the massacre; only three escaped that carnage.

Dr. Shackelford eventually returned home to Courtland, Alabama. To his surprise, his funeral service had already been held. During a welcome home ceremony in his honor, he tearfully recounted the last days of the young men he had led to Texas including his son and nephews

Doctor James A. Barnard, born in Canada, was

practicing medicine in what was then the small town of Chicago, Illinois. In 1835 he heard of the Texas uprising against tyranny and offered his services. He explained his decision to go to Texas as follows:

"They were in arms for a cause that I had always been taught to consider sacred, viz; Republican principle and popular institutions. They had entered into the contest with spirit and were carrying it with valor."

He closed his office and, in the company of two like-minded young men, set off for Texas on December 14, 1835. Eventually meeting Captain/Doctor Shackelford on the Texas coast, he joined the Red Rovers. The company was shortly ordered to report to Goliad/La Bahia for duty with Colonel James Fannin.

Like his friend, Jack Shackelford, James Barnard was an avid observer and writer. His memories are detailed in "Dr. J.H. Barnard's Journal, from December 1835, including the FANNIN MASSACRE, March 27, 1836." (see Recommended Reading)

The following is taken from his Journal and describes the duties he and Dr. Shackelford performed, as captives, for the Mexican wounded in Bexar following the Goliad massacre:

"We have two colonels and a major and eight captains under our charge, who were wounded in the (Alamo) assault. We have taken one ward of the hospital under our charge. Their surgical department is shockingly conducted, not an amputation performed before we arrived, although there are several cases even now, that should have been operated upon at the first, and how many have died from the want of an operation is impossible to tell..."

Barnard also served in the Texas Army at Galveston, Texas, briefly in 1836, then moved to Fort Bend County in 1837. There he served as county clerk from 1838 to 1839. In 1841, he married Mrs. Nancy N. Danford, moving to Goliad where he resided until 1860. On a visit back to Canada the next year, Dr. Barnard died.

Barnard's philosophic last journal entry summarizes the previous defeat at Goliad while reflecting on the victory at San Jacinto and its aftermath:

"Strange and unaccountable have been the vicissitudes of fortune. Surely no mortal can tell what the morrow may bring forth. Our disastrous battle was succeeded by the glorious one at San Jacinto. While we sorrow for the loss of our comrades, our brethren from San Jacinto, flushed with triumph, are passing by in pursuit of our discomfited enemies, and when we recall to mind our hard, hard fate, prisoners of a merciless foe, we now hear that the same foes are in our power, and the last, though not least among them, this modern Nero, the instigator of the war, the dreaded destroyer, the author of all the atrocities committed in Texas, the once great but forever fallen Santa Anna."

Doctor Joseph E. Field succinctly summarized his background:

"...having resided several years in the Southern States, without succeeding in business to my entire satisfaction, I was induced by some newspaper representations of Texas, to visit that famed, but as yet, little-known region of the West. I lived in the vicinity of Brazoria and Matagorda, something more than two years...At the breaking out of the war and when an army was wanted, I was among the first the first to come forward in support of the rights and interests of that community."

Of the three surgeons, Doctor Field participated in the most revolutionary struggles: Gonzales, Conception, Bexar and Coleto.

In his slim volume, "Three Years in Texas" (see Recommended Reading), Field wrote about his "accidentally" being at the famous October, 1835, battle of Gonzales, "the Lexington of the Texas revolution":

"Being accidentally in the vicinity of Gonzales, at the time when a force of one hundred and fifty Mexican soldiers came to the above place, and demanded of the Alcalde of that place, the surrender of a cannon belonging to him, I promptly complied with the call of the citizens of the place for aid, and though our number at the time of the demand was only eighteen, we returned an answer to them to come and take it.

"On the morning of the sixth of October, we, under the command of Col. J. More, a force nearly equal to theirs, crossed the Guadalupe River, and attempted to surprise them in their camp, but were unable by reason of a very thick fog, which prevented our discovering their exact position until they had taken the alarm, fled and assumed a position on an eminence about one mile distant.

"When the fog was so far dissipated, as to enable us to see them, we sent them a challenge to come and try the right of property by powder and ball. But they declined and being mounted, while we were on foot, we could only send them a parting benediction from the mouth of the cannon they had come to take."

Field described the intensity of the fight within Bexar (San Antonio):

"With crow bars we perforated the walls of the houses toward the square, making pot holes, through we kept up a constant fire at them…In this way, and in opening communications with each other by means of ditches, we spent the day, the besieged keeping up a raking fire through the streets by day and by night."

Field arrived at La Bahia on the night of March 6, 1836. His unpleasant journey of seventy miles was alone and through "a country so beset with Indians, as to make it necessary to ride by night."

Reporting to Fannin, he found everyone preparing to vacate the presidio and retreat to Victoria in accordance with General Houston's order. "… after having marched nine miles," Field remembered, "we were overtaken and surrounded by a Mexican force of eighteen hundred, most of whom were mounted."

After Fannin surrendered his surrounded command "at discretion" to Urrea the next day, those prisoners able to walk were marched back to La

Bahia. Dr. Field, Fannin and Dr. Barnard remained at Coleto "encamped upon the ground."

Mexican Colonel Holzinger, in charge of their guards, asked Fannin who was his best surgeon and Fannin pointed at Field. On his return to La Bahia, Doctor Field was interned with the others in the chapel where "our only resting place was the bare ground, offensive with filth."

Colonel Holzinger later assigned Field, along with several wounded Mexican officers, to a house outside the walls of the presidio. "Our whole time (the surgeons)," Field continued, "was taken up in dressing the Mexican wounded. All our medicines, surgical instruments and bandages were taken from us; and none of *our* soldiers had their wounds dressed, except a few by Major Miller."

The next morning was Palm Sunday and the beginning of the organized massacre of the prisoners by order of Santa Anna. "Being outside of the Fort I was an eye-witness to but a small part, but was informed what was going on."

Doctor Field found most of his fellow prisoners, involved in caring for the Mexican wounded, hesitant to join him in a later escape attempt. "They all believed it impracticable and that a failure would be attended with immediate death." Eventually he found a German named Vose who was willing to make the attempt. The two succeeded in reaching the San Antonio River one dark night and fording it. Since his companion could not swim, Field constructed a raft and towed

Vose across their next river, the Colorado. On the eleventh day, they encountered a Texas soldier who told them about the recent victory at San Jacinto. They continued to Velasco by mid-May where Field asked for and received a furlough to return to the U.S.

A SUMMARY OF THE
TEXAS CASUALTIES
(Source: Wikipedia)

BATTLE/ SKIRMISH	COMMANDER	KIA	WIA	CAPTURED
Agua Dulce	Grant	12-15		6
Alamo	Travis	182-257		
Bexar/Bejar	Austin	35		
Coleto	*Fannin	10	60	
Concepcion	Bowie	1	1	
Goliad	*Fannin	428-445		
Gonzalez	Moore	0		
Lipantitlan	Westover	0	1	
Refugio	Ward/King	31		107
San Patricio	Johnson	16		21
San Jacinto	Houston	11		

TOTAL OF ABOVE	726-821	62	134
FANNIN TOTAL OF ABOVE	428-445	60	
FANNIN PERCENTAGES OF ABOVE	59-54	97	

Printed in the United States
By Bookmasters